CW00841308

Dreaming of Retiring to the Costa Blanca?
Volume 2

Your New Life Starts Here

.

Table of Contents

Introduction

When I finished "Dreaming of Retiring to the Costa Blanca" in 2014, I raised my fingers from the keyboard with a contented sigh. It would, I thought, be quite a few years before I needed to think about an update. After all, this is Spain. Much as I love Spain, even I have to admit that things move at a slower pace here. A lot may happen, but it tends to take its time. Lots of time.

Oh, yes?

Purely for my own interests, I keep an eye on the local and national press, to make sure that there is nothing going on that will affect us as a family. I also get regular updates from a number of professional organizations, check a number of Government websites, and get several newsletters from my own accountant/gestor. And in the past year, I think more has happened that has a bearing on expats in Spain than has cropped up in the entire ten years we have lived here. Add to that the massive amount of feedback and requests for further information that I have received - for which, many thanks - and I realised that it was time to issue an updated volume.

All of the information in Volume 2 is brand new; there are no repeats from Volume 1 except for the Tables relating to Inheritance, where I felt it necessary to add the information again or the text would not make sense. Some of the new information is - I hope! - both useful and interesting to anybody who is considering living here. Some of the new legislation is essential reading, and for once it is almost entirely beneficial to us ex-pats, or wanna be ex-pats. Thanks to the feedback I have received, I also realise that I left quite a lot out of Volume 1, having made the error of forgetting that I live here and what I take for granted is often exactly what people want to know who are at the thinking of moving over here stage.

I should also make the point that there has been no better time to consider buying in the last seven years; the pound is at a high against the euro at the moment, and this looks like holding for at least a while, fingers crossed! A few years ago, there was almost parity between the pound and the euro, whereas as I type you should achieve around €1.40 to the pound. Very beneficial indeed for forward currency transfers, and a delight when it comes to the cost of living here.

And finally, deepest apologies to those readers who live outside the UK. I have had feedback from people as far apart as the USA and Canada, and even Australia, who are interested in moving to the Costa Blanca. If I tried to include legislation and information world-wide, this would rapidly turn into an encyclopedia, so if you live outside of the UK, please forgive me. I hope that much of the information is still applicable to you.

So here it is; Volume 2 of "Dreaming of Retiring to the Costa Blanca".

And as always, if there is anything you think I have missed out, or would like further information about, please feel free to drop me an e-mail at yvonnebartholomew@telitec.com. I can´t promise to come up with an answer but I will always do my best to help.

Chapter One

Will I Like It There?

I received more feedback on the lines of "Is the Costa Blanca really for me?" than almost anything. And out of all the questions I received, this is by far the most difficult one to answer. Because of these two factors, I have dedicated quite a lot of space to considering the ins and outs of living here.

Of course, upping sticks and moving to another country is a huge decision - literally a life-changing event - so naturally you want to be as sure as you possibly can be that you are doing the right thing for you and for your family. You can, of course, go back to your home country if you find it's not for you, but that is likely to be an expensive decision, so best to get it right first time.

Why is it a difficult question to answer? I love it here, don't I? Wouldn't dream of moving back to the UK? You betcha! But I'm not you. I don't have close family in the UK - no children or Grandkids to worry about. Nor do I worry about problems with the language; I give it a go and if I get it wrong more often than not the patient soul I'm talking to will help me out. I'm happy to drive over here, and have got used to the idiot cyclists who pedal five abreast and go through traffic lights, and the fact that Spanish drivers never seemed to learn how to reverse, so if the space is narrow it's up to me. Nor do I mind the intense heat we get for seven or eight months a year. I now take it for granted that I can't do a "one stop shop"; if I want paracetamol or cough medicine I have to go to the pharmacy; if I have visitors who want cigarettes, then they have to go to the tobacconist to buy them. I know that there are certain things that I took for granted in the UK that are simply not available to me in Spain (Lanacane, Dettol, Savlon to name a few, and the hunt for decent size clothes still drives me mad).

So why on earth do I and my husband love it here so much?

It suits us. The lifestyle is right for us, and we soon realised that those areas that were not right were not going to change for us, but rather that we were going to have to make the changes. Fair enough; nobody asked us to move here, did they?

And I think this is the most important point to bear in mind if you are seriously thinking of moving over here. This is not the UK. It is never, ever going to be like Britain with better weather. If that is what you are looking for, then forget it. Do not make the move. Stay in the UK and holiday here. Even in areas where there is a high percentage of British residents (Torrevieja in the south, and Orba in the north, for instance) it is nothing like Britain. This is Spain, in all its glory, and it is not going to change for you, me or anybody else.

Point made? I hope so! I have seen so many people move over here, expecting the Costa Blanca to be just like a "home from home" only to be bitterly disillusioned when it is not, that it really is worth saying, over and over again.

OK, so if I have all these annoying areas to contend with, why do I like it so much? What is there here that will make *you* happy?

Pros and cons.

Prime under the "**pro**" heading is the culture. And by "culture" I do not mean the Sunday Supplement Lifestyle ethos; in Spain, that is largely under the "cons" column. I mean the day-to-day way of life.

The pace of life is, undoubtedly, slower. Unless, of course, you live in the very center of a vibrant and lively town like Benidorm, where the nightlife goes on forever. Generally, life outside the big holiday areas is s-l-o-w, and is all the better for it. You have worked all your life to get to the stage where you can enjoy yourself, so sit back and do just that! There is little pressure and less stress. The buses may not run entirely to the timetable (although they generally do) but are you going to worry if it's ten minutes late? You will have to allow an extra half hour when you take Rufus out for a walk, simply because you will be expected to stop and chat with the neighbours. I have to admit, on our Urbanization it's the done thing to stop car-to-car and have a word with people you haven't seen for a few days; even on the very narrow and very steep access road. This only drives holiday-makers mad; those who live here wait patiently. Of course they do, they know perfectly well it will probably be them doing the same thing tomorrow.

You will also find that there is simply more courtesy on the Costa Blanca. It's the done thing to call out "Buen Dias" or "Buen Tardes" ("Good morning" and "Good Afternoon") whenever you join a queue in a shop. Everybody will call out "Good Day" back, and I often wonder if the Spanish think us foreigners very rude when we don't do it. Try that in the queue in Boots and see what you get! On the other hand, you will also find that you appear to get a lot of queue jumpers, which inevitably leads visitors to get cross and consider the Spanish extremely rude. Not so! What happens is that a little old lady comes into the Butchers, and is shocked to find there is a long queue. She checks to see who is last, and then goes about the rest of her shopping. When she is ready to return, she checks for the person who *was* last in the queue and then takes her rightful place behind them, in spite of the fact that a further six people have now joined the queue. This is perfectly normal and accepted behavior.

And as for the so-called "mañana" culture? Apart from builders, (who tend to tell you what timescale they think you want to hear, out of sheer politeness. We had an extension built a few years ago, for which our Spanish builder quoted a timescale of 6 weeks. It actually took him 17 weeks. But he did an excellent job) you may be amazed at delivery times. It is perfectly normal to buy a large item like a fridge or a television, and have it delivered the same afternoon. If it has to be the next day, the shop is likely to apologise for the delay.

And you do get used to the sunshine! When the weather is bad, Spaniards take it personally. In order to alleviate the pressure, supermarkets and shops quite often lay a table with flasks of coffee and packets of milk and sugar, to comfort their suffering customers. Around Christmas, a lot of small shops have bottles of liqueur or sweets on the counter, for customers to help themselves to as a gift and "thank you" for their custom. Many independent shops - whether you buy anything or not - will press a small Christmas gift on you; nothing expensive, perhaps a sprig of mistletoe or a little token for the Christmas tree. But it really is the thought that counts! And more often than not, even when you have splashed out a whole €10 on a 3-course Menu Del Dia, you will be offered a liqueur on the house. Nice? It certainly is.

And get used to quite a lot of bluntness. Trying clothes on? If you are in a communal changing room, or pop out to ask your other half ("Media Naranja"; yes, honest!) what they think, then you are quite likely to get some advice from any Spanish ladies who happen to be about. And they don't mince their words; if they think something doesn't suit you, they will tell you so. In fact, you need to get used to quite a lot of honesty here in Spain. I am, shall we say, "traditionally built". I had to have a hernia repair last year, and had a resultant problem with internal bleeding. My Surgeon told me bluntly that this was common amongst "people who had too much belly fat." He wasn't trying to upset me, it's just the Spanish way. They see nothing impolite about stating the obvious!

And generally, here in Spain family life is still paramount. If you get a child having a tantrum in the supermarket, they are highly unlikely to be Spanish. It's the exception to find children misbehaving rather than the rule. Very young children are taken to restaurants and are expected to choose what they want to eat, and then cope with it themselves. Quietly. With no help from Ipads, computer games or mobile phones. They are expected to join in the conversation, and enjoy their food. Along with their siblings, parents and often grand-parents.

All sound good to you? Excellent!

I should also add that the Costa Blanca is generally a safer place to live than the UK. There is crime; even here on our peaceful Urbanization we have burglaries. And the whole of the Northern Costa Blanca has just been shocked to the core by a terrible double murder in Jalon, where formerly the most exciting thing that ever happened was when two motorists refused to back down on the narrow access bridge. But. This hit the headlines simply because it was so very unusual. I do not hesitate to walk my dog in the dark here. My husband and I are happy to go out for dinner, and take a stroll around the villages afterwards. Even before we left the UK nearly ten years ago, we would have hesitated to do either, and we lived in a small market town. There is violent crime in the major cities, but even here it is rarer than the UK. And the police and Guardia Civil are inevitably prompt, polite and helpful if you do have a problem. And, bearing in mind that you are considering retiring here, it is a fact of life that the Spanish are far more respectful and helpful towards the elderly than you would find in Britain. Yes, I know. You are not elderly. Neither am I, but unfortunately we are both being propelled inexorably in that direction.

Enough said!

If you are into sport, you will also find the Costa Blanca an excellent place to retire. Tennis, padel, crown green and ten-pin bowling, bicycling, surfing, diving, and swimming - all are available everywhere, year round. There are also more excellent golf courses than you could shake a stick at. If you want to watch rather than participate, even the smallest of towns has a local football team, who attract spectators from all nationalities.

A major worry seems to be that you may not know what to do with your time (a subject which it appears quite a number of people coming up to retirement age has a problem with). Firstly, bear in mind that you are living here, you are not on holiday. As a result, you will need to do everything that you would do if you were retired in your home country - shopping, cleaning, gardening and DIY etc. When you've finished eating out, enjoying the sunshine and exploring your new country, there is any number of voluntary organizations who would love to have you help them. These range from the Samaritans to cat and dog sanctuaries to charity shops to home visits for the elderly and cancer patients. All the local papers carry repeated requests for help, if you find you have spare time, they would love to hear from you. There are also branches of UK and world-wide organizations such as the Lions and the Masons, scattered throughout the Costa Blanca.

I have received a number of questions about health care, and I am pleased to be able to confirm that here on the Costa Blanca the health service - both national health and private - is superb. I am sure there must be instances where problems arise, but both my own family and all our friends and neighbours have nothing but praise for the system. To give you an example, if we need to see our GP I go on line and make an appointment. In a few key strokes, I have his full schedule for the coming week, and I can make an appointment on a day and time that suits us. I have never (and as my husband is

Type 1 diabetic with an associated raft of health problems, we do make good use of the system) failed to make an appointment for the next day; quite often if I go on line early I can get an appointment for the same day. If you are not computer literate, don´t worry - you can either ring or go into the Health Center for an appointment. If you need a referral to the hospital, the doctor is usually able to go on line to get the referral for you whilst you are there; by the time you get to Reception, the appointment is ready for you. Private health insurance is relatively cheap, and absolutely superb. If you are eligible to receive state healthcare, all pre-existing medical conditions are covered. If you have to go private, many of the companies offer at least limited cover for pre-existing conditions.

All sounds wonderful so far? It is. But there is a downside, largely depending on the sort of lifestyle you have in the UK. So, the **cons**....

Your family situation is going to have a major impact on how happy you will be here. If you have children and grandchildren who are close to you, **please** consider that they will no longer be on your doorstep. Even if they live a couple of hours drive away in the UK, they are still within contacting distance. Remember, if they want to see you here, flights have to be booked, plans have to be made. Even with a flight time of only a couple of hours, it´s still likely to be a day's journey factoring in airport runs as well. At both ends. You are simply not going to see children and grand-children as often as you took for granted in the UK. I know, there is Skype and webcams, but it's not the same. We have seen so many good neighbours and friends who have gone back to the UK simply because they found they missed their family so very much. The ties that bind are not easily broken, and you really must factor it in.

And if you are newly retired from a high-powered job, or are used to living a frenetic lifestyle with a bulging diary and every second accounted for, please think twice before you consider moving here. The pace of life *is* slower. It is far, far more relaxed than the UK. You will, undoubtedly, make new friends here, but social life on the Costa Blanca tends to center around meals out at local restaurants, with the occasional BBQ or party on somebody's terrace to celebrate a special event, or when friends are over from the UK. Ladies who lunch are not exactly unknown, but it just doesn't happen as often as it does in the UK. Wild parties that go on into the small hours are generally relegated to those lunatic holiday makers, and - be warned! - if they happen too often in residential areas, they are likely to result in a complaint to the Guardia, who **will** act on behalf of sleep-deprived locals. In urban areas (by which I mean on Urbanizations and residential areas in towns generally) most cafes and restaurants close at twelve at the latest, unless there is a special event for which they have permission to stay open later. If there is a recognized fiesta taking place, all that is totally forgotten, of course. In my own small town, the entire town stays open all night for the major fiestas, with the fun starting at around midnight and finishing on the stroke of eight - next morning! But these are exceptional events, not every week-end.

And if your idea of a fun way to spend a week-end starts with an intensive morning of shopping followed by a visit to an art gallery or museum, with a trip to the cinema or theatre in the evening, forget it. This is simply not going to happen on the Costa Blanca.

To begin with shopping. There are shopping centers, which generally are not as big as the Malls in the UK and elsewhere. But these are almost inevitably located well outside the city center, and you need a car to get to them. And Sunday is generally (with the normal caveat of unless you live in a major city or tourist area) still a rest day on the Costa Blanca. Virtually all shops (including supermarkets and local shops) close all day Sunday, as do the large shopping centers. All you are likely to find open on a Sunday for most of the year are a sprinkling of British supermarkets and petrol station shops. All shops are also closed on Bank Holidays, local holidays and Saints´ Days. And trust me; there are a lot of those! Local shops generally still adhere to the principle of closing for a couple of hours in the afternoon for a siesta. Plays havoc with normal, British shopping patterns, at least until you get used to it. Things get a little more relaxed in the main summer holiday season, when some supermarkets and shopping centers do open on Sundays, but it´s not guaranteed. And don´t forget you will need to keep some cash in your pocket; there are hardly any cash machines outside the banks, and not all local bars and restaurants have the facilities to accept credit and debit cards.

Also beware; if you are even slightly larger than average, you will find it difficult to buy clothes. Most Spanish are smaller than us hefty English, and so sizes are comparably small - and short! I have seen size 12 clothes labeled as "Extra Large" before now, and if you have big feet, you have problems. You will be lucky to find a woman's shoe size much bigger than a 6. Men's clothes are equally difficult to find in large sizes. I should give a word of praise here to C & A, who have branches in many shopping malls, and who not only stock clothes in a wide range of sizes but also have "Grande" ranges for both men and women. The only problem is that you will have to push me out of the way to get to them …

And for the culture vultures; well, it´s not exactly a desert, but it´s not lush either. Most towns have a cinema, but outside the larger towns the films will be in Spanish, without so much as a hope of sub-titles. There are theatre groups, but these - again, outside the very large towns - tend to be amateur dramatic productions, and you will be lucky to find more than perhaps three or four productions per year within reasonable traveling distance. There are concerts with well known names, but for these you are likely to have to travel to Alicante or Valencia. Benidorm Palace doesn´t exactly qualify as "culture", but they do have excellent shows and often visiting celebrities of very high quality. There is also always something going on at a local bar somewhere - quite often, names that used to be big in the rock scene quite a few years ago. But nothing whatsoever that compares to the range of entertainment you would expect in virtually any city in the UK.

Likewise art galleries tend to be local, showcasing local talent. Nice to visit, but they are certainly not going to take you all day. Museums, also, tend to be locally biased.

And I really must mention the weather. Winters on the Costa Blanca are very mild compared to the UK, but the sun does not shine all year. It can be cold, and damp. Admittedly, no snow, (we last had a bit of snow about five years ago; people were so astonished that they came out of offices and shops to have a look. The last snow before that? Around thirty years ago) no ice, no frost. But when it rains, it puts Britain to shame. And the Costa Blanca generally can get very high winds. Most Spanish property is built to try and keep you cool in summer, so you have very high ceilings and lots of windows. In winter, property takes a lot of heating to keep cosy. We have oil central heating, and we use it. After a year or two, you really do get used to the milder climate and look at those mad tourists wearing shorts in January in total disbelief. And in summer? Well, it's official. Alicante Province is now the driest inhabited area in the world, beaten only by the Attacama desert, and that doesn't exactly have a huge population. Spring and summer is not just hot, it's sizzling. We have temperatures in excess of 40°C on our terrace day in and day out for months on end. Nights when the temperature stays at 30°C +. Days when you long for a bit of rain, or even a cloud. It might sound wonderful when you are in the UK in the middle of a snowstorm, but trust me, you do have to get used to it. And it´s not for everybody; we have had neighbours who just could not stand this sort of heat, it actually made them ill, and eventually they retreated back to cold, grey Britain. Gratefully.

Generally, there is plenty going on, all through the year. Lots of fiestas. Lots of local events. There is no shortage of things to do, places to go. But it´s horses for courses.

If you long for a bit of peace and quiet, for some space of your own and lots of nice places to eat, at incredibly reasonable prices, with good weather and what is still a very moderate cost of living in a relaxed, family orientated environment, then welcome to the Costa Blanca. You will love it.

On the other hand, if you want a fast lifestyle, with a huge choice of events at your fingertips and a wide variety of shopping, fine dining and entertainment available day and night, don´t bother. Unless you are prepared to live in one of the big cities, this is simply not going to happen. And even there, the ethos has little of the rush and push of the UK. I promise you, if you move to a "normal" town or urbanization on the Costa Blanca and you are anticipating this sort of lifestyle, you will be bored stiff within a month. Think of it in terms of moving from the center of London to a sleepy village in the middle of nowhere. You have to travel to even do serious window shopping. There are no theatres on your doorstep. No choice of cinemas. Even the art galleries and museums are rustic. Oh, and you have to use a car to get anywhere; no all-night public transport links. And even all your wide circle of friends has suddenly disappeared; no chance of ringing up and arranging an impromptu get together - unless, of course, they are happy to hop on a plane at a moments notice. Doesn't sound enticing? In that case just come on holiday here, and then you can go back home at the end of your fortnight.

But don't move here permanently!

Chapter 2

Where in the Costa Blanca?

Something else I forgot to discuss in any detail, and clearly something people considering moving here want to know about.

Basically, the Costa Blanca is divided very roughly into two halves, logically enough, North and South. The South is hotter and drier, with less greenery. The price of property tends to be somewhat cheaper in the South than in the North. The North is (comparatively) cooler, but is still very hot in summer, and greener. Depending on where you want to be, property in the North ranges from slightly more expensive than the South to a hefty 40 - 50% more expensive.

So, what locations are out there?

I would strongly advise that the only way to find where is right for you is to come here for an extended visit, and roam. If at all possible, come at different times of the year to get a flavour of both the summer heat and the winter weather. I would put money on the fact that as soon as you see the right place for you, you will know it immediately. But, as so many people have asked, what is available?

Very, very briefly, this is a much-compacted guide to the North and South. Come and look for yourself, but at least this gives you an idea what to expect.

This is also probably as good a place as any to clear up one major misconception - again, a question that has arisen frequently. It is *not* the case that most Spanish in the Northern Costa Blanca speak only Valenciano. You may find that elderly people in the smaller villages either only speak Valenciano, or prefer to speak it, but generally most of the population of the Costa Blanca North also speaks Castilian Spanish - the stuff you learn in school. Many younger people learn English as a second language in school, and would love to try it out on you! In fact, I often find that I start a conversation in Spanish, only to discover after a few sentences that the person who I am talking to has switched to English, to improve their own language skills. This has the distinct drawback of making me very, very lazy about improving my Spanish.

So here are a few suggestions of places you might like to take a look at. Some of these are popular holiday destinations, and are relatively well known. Others are far more obscure, but none the less wonderful places to live in if you have made the decision to move here.

Costa Blanca North

The dividing line is Alicante Airport; anything North of the airport is deemed (here, at least, if not officially) to be the Northern Costa Blanca. And to be perverse, I am starting at the very top and working back down towards Alicante. Anything much beyond Gandia in the north is generally regarded as Costa Azahar ("Orange Blossom Coast"). Still lovely, but strictly not the Costa Blanca.

Generally, the North is greener and somewhat cooler than the South. It is also much more mountainous. The North is still quite traditionally Spanish, and generally new build has been restrained to respect existing property. Apart from Benidorm and Calpe, skyscrapers are few and far between.

The furthest point north is around **Gandia**. Gandia is a lovely, medium sized town, but very Spanish! If you want to live here, then some Spanish is definitely recommended. It has a beautiful center and is very historic (Gandia is actually home to the infamous Borgia popes, and it has some fabulous medieval buildings and an excellent museum in the center) and also has superb beaches. Property around Gandia is still relatively inexpensive, probably because fewer ex-pats have found it yet.

This area is full of orange groves and majestic mountains in the background. The sandy beaches are excellent and uncrowded. Inland is pretty with probably the best known town being **Xativa**, which is a beautiful medieval town with a wonderful castle. It is very hilly, and gets quite a lot of tourists, but is still very traditional and property is way cheaper than along the coast

Heading south on the coast you go through **Oliva**. This is a fairly big and bustling town. Plenty of shops, restaurants and bars and a good weekly market. Good beach as well. Very large Urbanization at Oliva Nova; not that cheap to buy property here. Appears to me to have more traffic lights per metre through the center than anywhere else in Spain.

Down a few kilometers from Oliva is **Pego** (I'm prejudiced, as this is our nearest "town", but it has plenty of shops, banks, bars, supermarkets etc. Again, some Spanish helps but you can get away without it). Quiet, apart from Market Day on Thursday when parking is impossible. Property is still relatively reasonably priced. No beach, as Pego is slightly inland, but there is a lovely sandy beach at Les Deveses, about ten minutes drive away. Basically Pego is a traditional town with a very Spanish feel.

El Vergel and Ondara are a little further along, and virtually run into each other. Both are nice, bustling little towns, and well worth taking a look at. Plenty of shops, bars and restaurants and property is reasonably priced in both. No beach, but one is easily available a few minutes drive away at Els Poblets. Both have markets, both are - like Pego - still working towns that do not rely on the tourist trade to make a living.

Moving down the coast slightly you come to **Els Poblets**. It′s bigger than you might think, as it meanders. A lovely little town/very large village. It has banks, bars, a pharmacy, supermarkets and several very good and very cheap restaurants. It′s also totally flat! And with a long but pebbly beach. Because it has plenty going for it, it′s popular with ex-pats of all nationalities (particularly Brits and Germans) and property tends to be more expensive than other towns in the area.

Then a slight detour to **Denia**. This is a proper, large, town, which has things like the regional Social Security Offices and Guardia offices (this is where you go if you live in the area and need documents such as your Residencia). It does attract lots of tourists in the season, but it is still a working town, rather than being totally tourist orientated. Property is quite reasonably priced. It has around 22 kms of glorious, sandy beaches, and all the facilities you would expect from a town rather than a village. Denia also has a large marina and port from which you can get a ferry across to Ibiza, Menorca and Majorca.

Inland from Denia is the Orba valley with lots of villages such as **Sagra, Orba, Benimeli and Benidoleig.** Sagra and Benimeli are very small with nothing but a couple of restaurants and bars each. Very pleasant, very Spanish. Both Orba and Benidoleig are much bigger, with a good choice of all the facilities. Both have big expat Brit communities; Orba´s entire population is 50% British! Very reasonable house prices, with a number of urbanizations to choose from. Also popular is **Beniarbeig**, which is a gorgeous smaller village, but rather more expensive than Benidoleig and Orba. Also in the area are **Sanet y Negrals**, (lovely, but the urbanizations are very hilly) **Tormos** (tiny), **Murla** (out towards Jalon; lovely village but expensive) with the popular Puerta del Valle Urbanization. And still inland, you find the slightly larger villages of **Benimaurrell, Fleix, Campell and Fontilles.** Fontilles is famous locally as it has a working leper colony (honest! It´s housed in a very beautiful complex of buildings in its own grounds, and you are welcome to take a look around - visiting times are displayed on the gate. You will be even more welcome if you leave a donation). Because they are inland, and have little in the way of facilities other than bars/restaurants and a village shop or two, these areas are much cheaper than nearer the coast.

The **Jalon Valley** area is breathtaking. No beaches as it´s away from the coast, but it is in the middle of the almond area, and it is so beautiful that there are organised walks to view the trees when they blossom in spring. Local legend says the almond trees were originally planted to keep a Moorish princess happy; they reminded her of her home. True or not, it´s a lovely story and when the trees are in full bloom you can well believe it. **Jalon** itself is a nice, small town with a fabulous, huge market on Saturdays. All the shops, bars, banks, restaurants etc that you could ever want, but it does get very busy on market day, and attracts a lot of tourists. Also in the area is **Pedregeur and Alcalali**, both bustling towns with Pedregeur being more of a working town, and a good deal larger. Villages in the area - **Lliber, Xalo and Parcent.** Prices - as the Valley is away from the coast - are surprisingly reasonable, with the exception of Murla which commands a definite premium.

To the south of Denia comes **Javea.** It´s a medium sized town, but without the working city feel of Denia. Fabulous beaches and port area, masses of bars and restaurants and plenty of supermarkets, two good state health centers. Excellent market. The main "industry" is tourism, and it is very popular with holidaymakers - especially Brits and Spanish - in the summer (go early to get a parking space). Still very Spanish overall and a very pleasant, family orientated resort. Property tends to be pricy as a result.

Inland from Javea are the small, working towns of **Gata de Gorgos, La Xara and Benitachell.** You can group all this lot together. Gata is an old town, with a lot of history and plenty of facilities. It has one HUGE urbanization, very reasonably priced indeed but check it´s for you before you buy. La Xara is busy and is just outside Javea. Gets relatively few tourists. Benitachell is now almost a suburb of Javea, but is proud to call itself a town in its own right and is very pleasant with plenty of facilities. Has a golf course on the outskirts, and an excellent crown green bowling club. Slightly less expensive than Javea itself.

The village of **Jésus Pobre** is between Javea (administratively it comes under Denia, but it is actually just outside Javea) and Denia, and is a very peaceful, smallish village. Quite expensive to buy property here, but quiet, pleasant and handy for Javea and La Sella Golf Course.

Moving along the coast is **Moraira**. Another lovely small seaside town, again very popular with tourists in the season. All the expected facilities and a good weekly market. Excellent sandy beaches. Not as expensive as Javea for property, but still a lot more expensive than the slightly inland areas. Inland of Moraira is **Teulada** (more of a working town, but very agreeable) and on the coast (well, it has 4km of coastline) the town of **Benissa**. Both have all the facilities you would expect from small towns. Teulada gets fewer tourists; Benissa is rather larger than Teulada and because it has a beach rather more tourists. Both are popular with ex-pats and property is still fairly reasonable in both areas.

Then comes **Calpe**, one of the Costa Blanca's most famous tourist destinations. Originally a small fishing village, Calpe is now a bustling, busy town (think big! Fine if you want to live in a city-by-the-sea) with lots of high rise hotels and apartments blocks dominating the skyline. Calpe also has the famous rock called the Peñon de Ifach which rises from the sea and can be seen from miles around. On either side of the Peñon are two excellent wide sandy beaches. As you would expect for a town that is based on tourism, prices are rather higher in Calpe itself. It does have a high percentage of Brits in residence, so also has a lot of British-orientated bars and restaurants.

Further south again is swanky, picture-postcard **Altea**, right on the coast and with spectacular views over the sea. Very, very nice but it is expensive to buy here. Expect hills full of whitewashed houses, winding cobbled streets and designer shops. Lovely, but very hard on the knees if you have arthritis. And equally hard on the purse if you want to buy in the area.

A little further down is **Alfaz del Pi** (also known as L'Alfas del Pi) with the beach area of Albir. Lovely small town, not as expensive as Altea, but not cheap either.

And then ……..**Benidorm**, the biggest tourist resort on the Costa Blanca. There's no escape from Benidorm. You can see it from miles away, and it seems to get bigger every month, in spite of a supposed ban on further building of skyscrapers. It is *huge*; big, brash and bustling all year around. However, it does have a lot going for it if you like crowds and don't want to bother learning a single word of Spanish. The beaches of Playa Levante, Playa Poniente, Playa de Mal Pas and Playa de Cala Finestrat are soft sand, very clean and excellent. Throughout the year the nightlife in Benidorm is legendary. If you want cheap, cheerful and noisy, this is the place for you.

There are plenty of hotels, cafes, entertainment, shopping and a number of fine theme parks for the family such as Terra Mitica, Aqualandia, Mundomar, Terra Natura and Aqua Natura. You can take a boat trip to La Isla de Benidorm, a small uninhabited island great for snorkeling. Go watch a show at the Benidorm Palace. Shop to your heart's content, and visit a different bar every day of the year - and then some.

But it isn't for everyone - there is a lot of difference between wanting to holiday somewhere, and actually live there! It is always busy, generally cheap and cheerful. Because of the tourist trade, property in and around Benidorm is priced at a premium.

From Benidorm inland you go past **La Nucia, Polop and Callosa d'En Sarria**. All nice areas, and within easy reach of Benidorm. Because they are slightly inland, property is cheaper than in Benidorm itself. Also in the area is **Guadalest**, a renowned Costa Blanca tourist attraction. Very beautiful, very historic, but busy and hilly. Further inland is the large town of **Alcoy**, (also known as Alcoi) famous for its many bridges and **Bocairent, Castalla, Ibi,**

Cocentaina, Albaida, Xixona and Ontinyent. Because they are inland, all of these areas are much, much cheaper than the beach resorts. Well worth looking at if your budget is restricted, or you're thinking initially in terms of a holiday home.

Just this side of Alicante is **Villajoyosa (including El Montiboli).** Famous for its chocolate factories! Also very dependant on a high tourist trade. Good town center with all the amenities and shops you would expect, lovely beaches. Property prices are quite high, probably as it is so close to Alicante.

After Villajoyosa there is a succession of similar beach resorts with high rise apartment blocks and hotels although fortunately nothing like as big as Benidorm! First there is **El Campello,** (the famous caves of Canelobre are just inland near Busot). It is a 20-minute tram ride from Alicante city, so excellent for shopping with no worries about parking. It also has a busy marina and fish market, and good beach. This is followed by **San Juan** (which is virtually a suburb of Alicante, about 8kms from the center). Still has its own "center" and the great advantage for legs that are no longer as young as they were of being very flat. But very expensive to buy here.

This takes us neatly to Alicante itself. Although I´ve included it in the Northern section, it actually has far more of a Southern Costa Blanca feel to it. The area around Alicante is quite barren and brown, and very, very hot in summer. The town is large (or at least, by Costa Blanca standards) and tends not to have a very large tourist presence. Most people arrive at the airport and immediately go elsewhere, which is a pity as Alicante is a very pleasant, easily navigated town, with excellent transport links and lots and lots of good shops, restaurants, bars, etc. It also has an excellent beach. If you want to buy here, look well to the outskirts, property in Alicante itself and its suburbs (or at least, in the "nice" areas) is breathtakingly expensive. Think €500,000 upwards for no more than a reasonable villa with a garden and pool, on an Urbanization well out of the center. Beachfront property in Alicante itself is in the €1,000,000 + + bracket. Ouch.

Southern Costa Blanca

For the purposes of this guide, "Southern Costa Blanca" is the portion of the Costa Blanca to the south of Alicante. The South is generally much flatter and drier and browner than the North. The beaches are excellent, as are the golf courses.

Unlike the North, which still has mainly traditional villages and towns, with plenty of space between them, the South is very built up, often consisting of relatively new build which sprang up in the building boom of around ten - twenty years ago. Many resorts are more international than Spanish. Comparable property can be a lot cheaper than in the North.

If you don´t mind being slightly inland, there are a lot of traditional, interesting small towns and villages set on the hills around the Alicante area. **Sax, Villena, Elda, Novelda, Petrer, Monovar, Monforte del Cid, Aspe, Yecla, Caudette and Jumilla** to name a few. All far more traditionally Spanish than the coastal resorts, and with good access to the facilities of Alicante. Property in these areas is still remarkably reasonable.

Major Expat populations can be found in **Villamartin, Cabo Roig, Rojales, La Zenia and Campoamor.**

Villamartin is probably the best known of the group. Slightly inland, it still has access to good beaches and a number of golf courses. Accessible from either Alicante or Murcia airports. All the infrastructure you would expect, but very busy in summer when there is a huge influx of golf tourists. Property prices are still very reasonable.

Cabo Roig, Rojales, La Zenia and Campoamor are all much of a muchness. All bustling holiday resorts, with plenty of bars, restaurants and shops. Perhaps not quite as busy and well known as Villamartin, but still mainly focused on tourism. Plenty of property available, most reasonably priced.

A little further south on the coast is **Santa Pola**. Whilst this is a tourist resort with good beaches, it is also a working town and so - unlike most of the resorts in this area - does not curl up and die in the winter. It also has history and tradition on its side, so is distinctly more Spanish in feel and appearance than most of the new resorts. Plenty of choice of property, but comparatively expensive for the Costa Blanca South.

Moving on again is **Rojales**. Slightly inland (10 minutes to the nearest beach) with good access to golf courses and airports. A nice, still very Spanish town. One unusual feature is the proximity to the Natural Park of the Lagoons; excellent for bird watchers! Also has a good weekly market. Good choice of property, but not as cheap as some other areas.

And down to the famous (or infamous, depending on your viewpoint) small town of **Ciudad Quesada.** This is a modern town only built in the 1970's. As well as being a resort, Quesada has a huge, permanent ex-pat population and is especially popular with the British. It's modern, busy and bland, but has all the infrastructure you could want and the added advantage that you will never need to speak a word of Spanish. Great if you want the weather and the cost of living without those difficult foreign bits. Property - particularly apartments - is still cheap.

And then we arrive at **Torrevieja**, probably the best known of the resort towns on the Costa Blanca South. Torrevieja is big and bustling, if not quiet so lively as Benidorm. Like Benidorm, it started out as a fishing village and grew. And grew. Very popular with tourists and residents alike. It is surrounded by salt lakes, which - it is claimed - makes the climate particularly beneficial for those who suffer from arthritis or rheumatism. The housing stock is huge, as there is an apparently endless supply of new Urbanizations, so you can take your pick at very reasonable prices.

The town of **Pilar de la Horadada** is set slightly off the coast but there are beach areas at Torre de la Horadada, La Colonia and El Mojon. Lots and lots of tourists and ex-pats alike! Lively and plenty of infrastructure. Prices are middling.

And so ends the whistle-stop tour of the Costa Blanca! North or South, you pays your money and you takes your choice. There are many, many smaller towns and villages than I have space to mention here; this is purely designed to give you a flavour of what is available, where.

Enjoy discovering which location is right for you.

Chapter 3

What Should I Bring With Me?

It really should have occurred to me to do a short chapter on this subject in Volume 1. The more so as it´s a perennial topic of conversation amongst ex-pats; "I really wish I had bought X with me." Or, "Do you know, I bought Y over and it´s stayed in the underbuild ever since?" Or even, "If you're coming over to visit with us this summer, do you think you could possibly bring XYZ with you, please?"

Yet another area where I have had a lot of requests for information!

There isn´t a great deal you can´t buy over here. But some of it is different to what you are used to. Some of it is more expensive. Sometimes there just isn´t the choice you are used to in the UK and elsewhere. Generally - particularly when you are looking at expensive removal costs - an area that is well worth considering.

To start with the small, everyday items. The bits and pieces you take for granted outside Spain. In the pharmacy (which is the only place you can buy anything vaguely medical - and I´m talking an aspirin upwards here) you **cannot buy** brands such as Germolene, Lanacane (either Anti-Chafing Gel or the normal, anti-itch cream), Savlon cream, or Buttercup Syrup cough medicine. There is nothing available that approximates to Lanacane Anti-Chafing gel. There is a gel with a local anesthetic in it, which is similar to Lanacane, but it costs around €13 for a small tube. Ouch! The alternative to Savlon cream is a clear gel (called Christalmina). It costs only a couple of euros, but I don´t find it as easy to use or as effective as Savlon. There are plenty of propriety cough medicines available, such as Benyln and Venos, but I have always been partial to Buttercup Syrup and I miss it! I have also never been able to find Dettol disinfectant or TCP. Either stock up before you move, ask willing friends and relatives to bring a bagful with them when they come, or stock up yourself when you are in the UK.

A word of warning if you are diabetic. If you are on the National Health system here, you will get vastly reduced prescription insulin, metformin, etc. But you cannot get either testing strips or needles on prescription; you have to pay full price for both. Needles are around €15 - €18, depending on the length, for a box of a hundred. Testing strips are made for Spanish machines, which measure blood glucose on a different scale to the UK. The Spanish strips cost around €20 per box of 50. My husband is diabetic and we still use his old testing machine, buying the strips in bulk off e-bay!

I should add that the good news in this area is that you can get most things over the counter in the farmacia, without a prescription. This includes virtually everything that would be a prescription item in the UK; take the box in if you have run out and ask for the Spanish equivalent. You used to be able to get antibiotics over the counter with no hassle, but there has recently been a move to clamp down on this, in an attempt to control over-use and anti-biotic resistance. I do like to have some antibiotics on hand, basically to save a trip to the doctor, and so I cheat. I tell the farmacia that my husband has a suspected tooth infection, and our dentist has told me to get antibiotics if it shows signs of getting worse. Not sure if they believe me, but it does result in a pack of antibiotics.

Moving on to kitchen equipment. You can buy most white goods over here, at similar prices to the UK. One minor annoyance is vacuum cleaners; I had an excellent Dyson Animal upright in the UK. As it was fairly elderly, we decided to leave it behind. I have since discovered that upright vacuums are a rarity over here; we now have a Dyson cylinder, but it's nowhere near as good as my old upright was. Either that, or Spanish dog and cat hairs are more difficult to vacuum up....

I also left behind a lovely American style fridge-freezer, as everybody told me that English fridge-freezers cannot cope with the heat in Spain. The compressors pack up quickly, I was told. Not worth paying a lot of money to move the whacking great thing. Oh, yes? Virtually all our neighbours bought their fridges and freezers across with them, and most are still going strong ten years later. When I asked about the reliability of them, I just got a funny look and was told that was what the regulator was for …. Doh!

For some unknown reason, I also persuaded myself that we would not be having roasts in Spain. So I gave my beloved spiked, stainless steel carving dish to a charity shop. I now find we have chicken far more frequently than we did in the UK, and that a piece of roast beef or lamb on Sunday is lovely in winter. And can I find a carving dish here? I cannot.

Another niggle is the kitchen bin. Seriously! You can find lots and lots in plastic, but I really, really want a decent, large sized stainless steel one. At least 50l capacity. Preferably with a flip lid, as I find the pedal variety break very easily. They do have them, in most DIY outlets. At a price. I have not seen one priced at less than €250. For that, I want a new oven, not a kitchen bin. If you have a decent one, bring it across with you (you can always pack delicate stuff inside it for transport across). Brabantia spares are available here, if you need them!

And lastly on the kitchen list …. Bread bins and biscuit barrels. They are very, very rare over here. I have no idea what Spanish housewives do with their bread and biscuits, but they certainly do not put them in a bread bin or biscuit barrel. If you have them, bring 'em with you.

All other gadgets, if they work and are not too elderly, you might as well bring them with you. Dead easy to change plugs, and no problem with incompatible electricity supplies. This also saves you having to buy everything all over again the minute you set foot in your Spanish property.

Furniture is a different matter again. There are lots of furniture shops. Lots of them sell a good range of furniture. But oddly enough, Spanish furniture often doesn't seem to do it, either for us Brits or the Germans. Perhaps it's because the Spanish tend to be smaller than us, but I find that upholstered Spanish-made chairs and sofas are too low for rising and sitting in comfort. (I should perhaps add that you will find Spanish toilets much lower than the English variety, but not a great deal you can do about that). Upholstered furniture also seems to be softer than the English variety. Lots of nice leather sofas, at decent prices, but far more difficult to buy a traditional 3-piece suite in leather. And I have to say that leather tends to be popular, as fabric furniture needs comparatively more cleaning because of the heat; to put it bluntly, you sweat more and your furniture suffers as a result. If you have teenage visitors, it's amazing how rarely they think it's a good idea to dry off properly from taking a dip in the pool, and sun-tan oils and lotions play havoc with fabric furniture. You can buy English style furniture from outlets, so worth keeping an eye open for one in your area. If you live in the South, there are literally hundreds of furniture shops in and around Torrevieja, which seems to have cornered the market in them. There is also a branch of DHS near Alicante, which will deliver furniture and beds, but only to the Costa Blanca south. Generally, if you have a decent suite in the UK, it's worth splashing out on removal costs and bringing it with you, as long as you make sure it will fit your new room, of course!

And the same goes for beds, and bedding. You can, of course, buy any size or shape of bed you want over here. There are outlets that sell nothing but beds, and many shops such as Ikea and Jysk also beds and mattresses. But. Just as Spanish clothes tend to be smaller in size than comparable English ones, so the beds are generally shorter. This may not sound much of an issue, but a couple of centimeters in length (the widths are generally the same) can mean the difference between a good night's sleep and your toes hanging over the edge and annoying you all night. And of course, mattresses are also shorter. And bedding - sheets and duvet covers - are normally also a bit shorter, which is very irritating when you are trying to fit them on to a standard English mattress. Of course, you are going to have to buy bedding at some point (I generally buy mine from Argos in Spain or Yorkshire Linen, which has branches all across the Costa Blanca) but if you have reasonably new beds, I strongly recommend bringing them with you. When you need a new bed or mattress (and even more so for the mattress - we nearly bought an expensive king size mattress recently, before it occurred to me to measure the old one. And yes; the new Spanish one would have been too short for the bed) it's worth sourcing a shop that sells English beds - more expensive than something you can pick up at a local outlet, but worth it.

Moving outside, spare a thought for garden tools and machinery. If you are going to have a garden in Spain, take your equipment with you. It's not that you can't buy tools and machinery here, you can. But the same sort of madness seems to overtake all of us when we move. We have a reasonable sized garden here, but it is tiny compared to the almost 1/3 of an acre we left behind in the UK. Probably because of the difference in size, we cheerfully decided we would have no use for hedge cutters, or the chain saw, or the garden shredder. And the new garden wasn't big enough to merit a garden vacuum, surely? And certainly not the extending tree-loppers. And no need to take basics like spades and rakes, was there?

We regretted it the first spring. We don't have a hedge to cut, but we do have quite a few trees that need pruning back severely each and every year. Likewise bushy shrubs. And we soon found that gardening in the dry Alicante soil was more like hacking coal out of a mine than just digging, so those expensive spades and forks would definitely have earned their keep. And the garden vacuum? Just bought our second one…

The truth is that gardening on the Costa Blanca can be an almost unending task. Everything seems to grow at double the pace it did in the UK; trees have to be pruned at least once a year, often twice. Bushes likewise. And leaves don´t just fall off in autumn, they do it throughout the year. And when it rains, everything runs amuck and genuinely can grow a couple of inches in a week or so. If you are going to have a garden, bring everything you find useful in the UK. Even if you only have a terrace or a substantial balcony, you are likely to find a power washer is very, very useful. When it rains, it often brings a very fine, very red sand with it - it comes from Northern Africa, and can´t wait to fall on your property. It´s very difficult to brush away, and if it´s a heavy deposit only a power wash does the trick efficiently.

Also outside, if you - or your Media Naranja - are into DIY, then bring every tool and piece of machinery you possess with you. Spanish villas and apartments tend to be high maintenance. The ceilings are high, to deal with the summer heat; great fun to paint! If you have aluminium double glazing, it wants to sweat in winter, which can play havoc with the plaster beneath the window. If you don´t have air bricks in your rooms, there is an ever present danger of unsightly black or green mould on your walls. Floor tiles are cool underfoot and easy to keep clean, but - particularly in kitchens and bathrooms - they crack and chip over the years. And of course, you have a lot of windows, which need cleaning and - if they are wood - varnishing regularly. Your window ironwork and iron railings need painting regularly .... Not trying to put you off; you soon get into a routine with regard to maintenance. And you can, of course, always pay somebody to do it for you. But if - like my husband - you would really prefer to do it yourself, then come prepared.

Most power tools are available over here, but there isn´t the selection you get in the UK. Odd things - like file sanders - are virtually unheard of. Items like cement mixers, scaffolding, power washers and wheelbarrows are relatively expensive. You also pay a premium for building wood - including chipboard and plywood. Not a lot you can do about the price of wood, of course, but at least you know what to expect. Some consumables you cannot get - decorator's caulk, for instance, is unknown. Paint and varnish - at least for the decent makes - are expensive compared to the UK. The Spanish equivalent of "No More Nails" ("No Mas Clavas") is expensive. There is isn´t the same range of fixings (particularly nails) that you take for granted in the UK. Well worth stocking up on if you are visiting the UK, especially if you are going via the ferry. Your English power tools will work perfectly well with a change of plug, or if you can´t be bothered just use an adaptor.

And a question I am asked often. Are furniture packages worth going for? It´s a "yes and no" answer. We bought a furniture package before we moved over, and it was of good quality and worked very well for us. But, we were not moving across immediately - we intended to rent our villa for holiday lets for around 3 years, which is what we did. When we moved across full time, we sold virtually the whole of the original package (with the exception of some garden furniture and a fridge-freezer, which are still going strong). Furniture packages will sort out your new home, literally down to the last teaspoon. From that point of view, they are excellent. But if you are moving across permanently, you are likely to want to bring at least some household items with you, so a full package would be unnecessary. It is also lovely to be able to browse around and pick up items when you want them. You are also restricted to what you can have in a package, although a word of warning - once the salesman gets you in the showroom, they are likely to try and persuade you to upgrade on major items like sofas and beds. The beds are definitely worth upgrading, as the basic ones in the package are often not what you would want for full time living.

Also, where people are selling their homes on the Costa Blanca to return to the rest of Europe, you will often find that they simply want to walk away from the property and its entire contents. The furniture may not be to your taste, of course, but more often than not it will do for the first few months, and gives you plenty of time to browse and order what you do want.

So, I´m afraid, it´s still a "yes and no". If you are buying a property with no possessions, and you want to rent it out for a while, a furniture package is well worth considering. If you want to move immediately and either bring some of your own furniture across or are inheriting furniture with the new property, don´t consider a package.

And on to the last - and biggest - "should I or shouldn't I" item. Your car. You can, of course, buy excellent cars over here. The prices are fairly similar to the UK; with Spanish-made SEAT´s in particular being cheaper than the UK. You can also buy a huge range of second-hand vehicles, but be warned; second-hand cars in Spain are relatively expensive, and that expense is not reflected in the price you will get when you trade in your old car to a dealer. There is also, oddly, not so much haggling when you buy a car over here. If the dealer is desperate to get a new model on the market, he may throw in a few desirable extras such as air-conditioning or a complete spare wheel (beware! Most new cars in Spain only come with one of those "good enough to get you to a garage" spare wheels - if you want a full spare wheel that can take the place of the damaged tyre, ask for it, and be prepared to pay for it as an extra) but otherwise there is not a great deal of movement from the showroom price. The same goes for trade in prices; you will be offered the book price, very rarely any more.

The exception to the "no bargain" rule is if you are trading in a very old car for a brand new one. The Valencian Government occasionally launches a "Plan Renove" which is an attempt to get the really ancient vehicles off the road. When these plans are in place, you are guaranteed an excellent package for your new car, but unfortunately they are usually aimed at trade-ins where the old car is ten years old and over. Some manufacturers will also offer a reduced price for new cars if you are happy to take their finance packages. Look at the details on the sale boards very carefully; you can find that your new car will be cheaper if you take out the garage's finance plan than if you are paying cash. Or at least it looks that way, until you calculate the finance costs ....

So, to bring or buy? Generally, unless you are very, very attached to your UK car, I would say sell it in the UK and buy new here. The reason is that it is both expensive and complex to re-register your UK car in Spain. And yes, you do have a legal obligation to re-register it. If you do not, you will find yourself in trouble if you are stopped at a road side check. You can also be discovered by Guardia who are simply doing a routine security drive around your Urbanization! This happened recently to some of our friends, who were unable to resist a bargain car on a trip to the UK. They came back to Spain with the car, and a couple of months later noticed the Guardia had stopped outside their villa and were taking a great interest in the car. They thought the police were simply admiring the car. Perhaps they were, but they also obviously made a note of the foreign import as a couple of months later they came

back and knocked on the door, demanding to know why it hadn't
been re-registered yet ....

Re-registering your non-Spanish car can cost several thousand
euros. You also have to submit a sheath of documentation, and pay
the fees for somebody to do the paperwork for you. All of this area
is covered in detail in Volume 1. You can do it yourself, but unless
your Spanish is excellent, all I can say is - "Good luck." You must
also have the headlights adjusted to conform to Spanish regulations.
And at the end of the process, you will still be driving a "wrong side
drive" vehicle, and are unlikely to get a great deal for it when you
finally decide to exchange it. Generally, easier and safer to buy a
Spanish registered vehicle when you get here. And with that in
mind, you may have been told that you have to be registered on the
"Padron" before you can buy a car in Spain. Officially, that may be
the case. Unofficially, I can confirm that we bought our first car
here - brand new and from a reputable Opel garage - long before we
got round to registering ourselves for the Padron. The salesman
assured us it would not present a problem and it didn´t.

Chapter 4

Scams!

Yes, I'm afraid we do have them in Spain. And often they are very well thought out. Please don't le this put you off considering moving here; I'm sure you will have something similar where you live now. I have included this section so you are aware - forewarned is forearmed.

All the normal internet scams will follow you here - the rich person who has died without heirs and wants to give you their money. The bank which appears to be telling you that there is something wrong with your account, and if you don't open the enclosed document your account will be frozen. The company which is sending you an unpaid invoice. Etc. The best one I have received recently was a very, very well produced effort which purported to come from PayPal. The only thing that gave it away was that it was not actually addressed to me by name; I forwarded it to PayPal fraud office and they confirmed it was a phishing attempt. Do what you always do with this lot, and simply delete them without reading or opening any attachments.

Unfortunately, we also have what are best described as "physical" scams. These range from dramas centered on your car to people actually turning up on your doorstep and trying to extract your hard earned money from you.

The following is a fair list, but more do turn up from time to time. If any of these appear to be happening to you, beware!

❖ You are driving along the motorway and a helpful car driver flashes you and waves at your tyres. You assume you have a flat and stop. Don't do it! As soon as you get out of the car, the "helpful" person who alerted you will draw up alongside and either distract you or offer to help. While they are doing this, another member of the gang will be sliding open your car door and helping themselves to anything they can find. This is particularly often aimed at women driving on their own. Never, ever leave your handbag on the seat in clear view. If you feel you must stop, lock the doors as soon as you get out of the vehicle.

❖ You are driving along and a car goes past and throws a raw egg at your windscreen. Whatever you do, do not flick your windscreen wipers on. This will cause the egg to smear all over your windscreen; you cannot see and will be forced to pull over and get out of the car to clean it properly. At that point, somebody will help themselves to anything you have in the car.

❖ You have stopped at a petrol station or supermarket, etc. You don't notice someone hovering near your car, but a couple of miles further on you find you really do have a flat tyre. When you pull over, a car with three or four helpful chaps stops to give you a hand. One of them helps you change your wheel, the other chats to your passenger. When you drive off, you find out that Helpful Person No. 3 has stolen your passports and your wife's handbag…

❖ You are loading your shopping into your boot when a flustered looking person comes up to you with a map in their hand. They ask you for directions; even when you tell them you have no idea, that you are a relative stranger here yourself, they persist. And of course, you don't notice their partner sneaking open your car door and helping themselves…..

Those are the favourites whilst you are driving. Then there are the shop scams….

❖ The favourite tends to be aimed at women, shopping on their own. A couple approaches you and browses the shelves near you. They then ask if you could possibly reach something down from a high shelf for them. Being naturally courteous, you do so. And while you are reaching up, a hand is slid into your handbag and your purse taken. In this case, they are usually after cash, not cards - it´s far from unusual to find your empty purse lying outside the shop when that horrible moment arrives and you get to the till, only to find you have no money.

❖ And for the chaps; never, ever keep your wallet in a trouser or shorts pocket. Pickpockets are very, very skilled. If you do find you have suddenly lost your wallet, do what a friend of ours did when this happened to him in our local Mercadona. He shouted - literally at the top of his voice - *"Bloquear las puertas, mi monedero ha sido robado" (Lock the doors, my wallet has been stolen)*. A moment later a helpful looking man he remembered bumping into him a little earlier nudged him and pointed to the floor by the cash tills, and there was his wallet, intact. Only slight problem was that our friend had not got that far, but who cared? It worked, and the thief got nothing.

And, sorry to tell you, the scammers even have the cheek to turn up on your doorstep in an attempt to deprive you of your hard-earned money.

❖ An absolute favourite is when a stranger knocks on your door. This is often a young, pretty woman. She will show you her ID, often purporting to be from a local charity and which looks totally genuine, and will then present you with a document - often written in Spanish, English and German - which is headed by a pathetic picture of a young child, obviously suffering from some life-threatening illness. The text tells you that this child is in terrible distress, and unless it receives life-saving treatment (usually in the USA) it will be dead within months. Any donation is appreciated. You will then find a clipboard thrust towards you with a list of your neighbours´ names and the amount that they have donated.

Don´t believe a word of it. These charity collectors are bogus; no genuine charity will

knock on your door and try to solicit funds. Smile
and say thank you, but no thank you. Shut the
door in their faces, they can be persistent.

❖ And then there is the bogus gas man scam. If you
have an indoor gas installation - either for your
hob or a gas fire - one of the state-approved gas
companies **will** knock on your door every 5 years
and ask to do an inspection of your installation.
The good guys will always have correct ID, but in
addition will be more than happy to wait quietly
whilst you ring the Policia Local to check them
out, which they will do very quickly, normally
arriving within a few minutes of a call. If you are
not due for an inspection, or have any doubts at
all about the identity of your "gas men", tell them
to go away. The real guys will come back, and/or
will be happy to give you an official telephone
number to get in contact with to confirm their
identity. The bogus ones will disappear very
quickly if you so much as mention the word
"Policia". Or, as was the case with us, one bogus
gas inspector dared to put his foot inside our drive
and was faced with our (extremely soft, but he
looks the part) Labrador showing his teeth and

growling. This one didn't even bother arguing, he simply disappeared. Rapidly.

And at the moment, that's the list of the favourites. Don't worry, just be aware. It happens everywhere, unfortunately. One last word on the subject; if you have not yet got your own car and are driving a hire company car, take extra care. What are presumed to be tourists are targeted far more frequently than residents. If you have to drive a hire car, it's a good idea to peel off those annoying decals that make their status so very obvious to everybody.

Chapter 5

When You Need a Little More Help

None of us like to think about getting older, but unfortunately it´s a fact of life. Of course, we all want to be independent for as long as possible, but there may come a time when you feel that totally independent living is either no longer practical, or you feel it would be rather nice to have a bit of help close at hand.

Spain differs greatly from the UK in its treatment of the elderly. I have not come across anything that resembles the sort of sheltered housing arrangements that are provided by local councils throughout Britain. It may exist, but if it does I cannot find it. Generally, because Spain is so very family orientated, the older members of the family are still looked after by children and grandchildren. There is what can be loosely called "Homes" for the elderly; these are called "Residencias" and are council run. Competition for a place in them is fierce; just because you are not Spanish it does not mean that you would be automatically excluded, of course, but finding a place in a Residencia might be difficult in any event.

So what is there out there when you need more support? The answer is lots! The downside, of course, is that generally you have to pay for it, but probably a lot less than you would be charged for something similar in the UK. The notable exceptions are those noble charities, staffed and run by volunteers, who will give at least short-term help when you need it most - generally after hospitalization. Details of these are given later in this chapter.

If you just need equipment - say, wheelchairs or walking support or a motor scooter - there are a number of companies from whom you can either buy or rent equipment. A few are listed below. Basic equipment may also be provided free by the **Help** organizations:

❖ **Mobility Equipment Hire and Rental**

The Hire Center

Wheelchairs, mobility scooters, walking frames and commodes for hire. Located at Calle Aviles Local 5 San Luis, 03184 Torrevieja. Tel: 966 786 225

Mobility Direct Spain

Wheelchair and mobility scooter rental in Calpe, Moraira, Javea, and Denia, Costa Blanca North. Situated in Teulada with a shop in Javea. Delivery to holiday rentals and hotels. Located at Calle Clementina Bertomeu 22, 03725 Teulada.

Nicholson Self Mobility Services

Claim to Specialize in stair lift installation in Javea, Denia, Moraira, and Benidorm. Suppliers of stair lifts by Stannah, Handicare Minivator and Otolift. At Calle Algarrobo 1003, Pedregeur, Alicante.

- Tel: 635 726 764
- Tel: 965 741 153

Active Life Equipment

Sales, service, rentals and repairs. A broad range of services including: scooters wheelchairs powerchairs bath lifts and daily living aids. Tel: 965 073 199

EasyHire Discount Mobility Costa Blanca

Hires 3 and 4 wheel electric scooters, walkers and electric wheelchairs. Service includes delivery in the Benidorm area and 24 hour availability. Contact at Aptd Correos 437, 03500 Benidorm. Tel: 966 445 812

If you need more help but would prefer to remain in your existing home, you can have a Carer visit. Generally, the Carer will be medically trained, but always wise to check this out first! Costs will vary according to what you need, and how often. There is also one charitable organization here on the Costa Blanca, which will offer limited home-help to ex-pats of any nationality - see below for full details of this excellent organization. Sadly, at present it is limited to the Torrevieja area. The various "**Help**" organizations also offer a (free!) helping hand with regard to equipment hire and in-hospital services - again, see below for full details.

The following companies provide paid services, but as always I am offering no recommendation whatsoever. Particularly here, where you are inviting a stranger into your home, moreover a stranger on whom you will depend, it is essential that you take up references and satisfy yourself regarding the service they provide and the people they are going to send to you.

I must make the point at this stage that the information contained in this chapter is purely designed to give you a flavour of what is available, and what you are going to get for your hard-earned money. The information given is provided by the organizations themselves, and **I am not making any recommendations, nor do I have any experience of any of the services or facilities on offer. I have not investigated any of the organizations referred to; they are quoted for information only**.

I have to admit that I was, initially, reluctant to actually give details of any specific organizations, as I am in no way connected with any of them and have no first-hand knowledge of their efficiency and care services. Nor have I accepted anything whatsoever from any organization or person to mention them here. However, I have been asked repeatedly what sort of care is available here on the Costa Blanca, and it occurred to me that there was very little use in trying to tell you what was out there without actually giving examples of what you can find, so I have taken a look at what is available, and included details - for information only.

If you are interested in any of the options, **please** investigate them carefully. You must ask for references, and take them up, and generally satisfy yourself that the service offered is suitable for you. Make sure that your money - and you - is safe before you make any investment, particularly in the residential complexes. And; there are lots more of them out there than I have space to consider here. This is no more than a sample of what you can expect, and the costs are only current at the time of writing (2015). This is your life and your money you are considering; whatever you do, make sure that you have made any and all enquires you think appropriate before moving forward.

Take care!

❖   **Care in Your Own Home**

Nursing Home Care

"A team of two ladies caring for you at home. Whether you are elderly, or have come home from Hospital. References can be provided as required. Hours 08:00-24:00. Call for further information. Tel: 622 794 882"

The 3C Care Agency

"Trained nurses and careers for all home help needs, including palliative, respite and post-operative care as well as specialized Alzheimer and dementia care nurses. Located at Villa Valencia Atzubia 2218, 03509 Finestrat. Tel: 671 856 875"

Mobile Care Assistant

"Home, hospital or respite care for the elderly, the infirm and people with learning or acquired disabilities. All aspects of care and support catered for. Covering all of the Costa Blanca and located in Orihuela. Tel: 660 222 778"

Servicio Ayuda a Domicilio Mosaic

"Home care and nursing from house cleaning to round the clock nursing care at home. Covering the area from Denia to Torrevieja. Located at Calle Plaza Jaume 1 10, 03720 Benissa. Tel: 619 216 270"

Open Door Foundation

"Home nursing, care and support service for older adults and the elderly with mental, physical and learning disabilities. Individual patient assessment and care packages, personal care, rehabilitation, respite care, sitting service and carers support. Tel: 666 911 545"

Prestige Nursing & Social Care Services

"Helping people to continue living in their own homes with greater ease. Services include trained nursing care, respite care, palliative care and domiciliary services. Calle Suiza 29 Edificio Belgico, 03502 Benidorm. Tel: 687 015 517"

❖ **Free Short-term Help after Hospitalization, etc**

Outstandingly, there is at least one organization that will offer unpaid short term help to ex-pats of all nationalities. This outstanding organization is **Help at Home Costa Blanca,** which offers:

"Free assistance to all nationalities, of any age, who find themselves in difficulty following illness, hospitalization, injury or respite assistance to carers of those with long term illness. We offer a little help to people in a time of need. This service is much needed, as expatriates from various countries do not always have the support of family members and have difficulty accessing this type of service due to language barriers nor can they afford nursing agencies.

We pride ourselves with the way we receive, respond and release to those in need of a little FREE help at home. When we receive enquiries, we respond within 24 hours and release the case when we have completed our care, usually within 4 / 6 weeks. Respite is offered for those who care for long term illness / conditions by caring volunteers, they offer friendship and support to those that need a break themselves. We need volunteers to help provide the much needed support for people with these debilitating conditions, MND, MS, CA, Alzheimers, Parkinsons, Dementia, Stroke and Huntingdons Disease, care is required longer and their Carers need respite. If you have a few hours a week and can help, wherever you live, contact 604 151 364 or email info.helpathomecb@gmail.com

We provide qualified NVQ carers, most of them with basic nursing experience, backed up by volunteers, funded by donations and sponsorship."

This service could be seen as loosely similar to the "District Nurse / Home Help" system in United Kingdom with the additional backup of non-medically qualified carers as required. Except, of course, this is a charitable foundation rather than state aid.

Membership and experience:

The charity consists of experienced Charity volunteers, qualified British / Spanish Nurses who provide Auxiliary Nursing care, NVQ Carers, Pharmacists, Drivers, Translators and a Spanish Advisor, plus over 120 enthusiastic volunteers.

Areas Covered:

Approximately 20 Km around Torrevieja, aiming to expand to more areas of Alicante/ Valencia as resources permit.

Phone: (+34) 604 151 364
Homepage: http://www.HelpAtHomeCB.org

Email: info@HelpAtHomeCB.org

❖   **Free Help in State Hospitals/Equipment Loan following Hospitalization**

Also free of cost are the excellent services provided by the various "**Help**" organizations around the Costa Blanca - details of these are given below. Generally, these groups´ volunteers are centered on the major national health hospitals. They provide translators for you in the hospital, can offer advice on items like respite care, and may even loan you equipment like wheel chairs, Zimmer frames and commodes free of cost (although a donation is always welcome) when you come out of hospital. They cannot offer nursing care, but they are wonderful organizations who will give you a helping hand just when you need it. My Spanish is reasonably good, but I invariably find my tongue gets in a twist when I am trying to explain to a doctor where it hurts; in these situations, the "Help" organizations are a life saver, as is the equipment loan service. This service varies from providing wheelchairs to raised toilet seats (and just try functioning without one of those if you have had a hip or knee replacement!) and most things in-between and is available for nothing more than the cost of a local telephone call.

All these organizations are registered charities, and whilst they do not charge, if you can make a donation for the services they provide they will be grateful.

HELP OF DENIA (Denia to Calpe)

http://www.helpofdenia.com

Office and Equipment Store: Telephone 966 427 044
e-mail: help:denia@gmail.com

Benitachell 664 573 360

Calpe 616 237 135

Denia 634 309 442

Javea 634 388 446

Teulada/Moraira 634 318 819

HELP OF BENIDORM

http://help-benidorm.com

Campello & San Juan (Chairman) 965638259

Equipment 965633332

Co-coordinator 965653479

JALÓN VALLEY HELP

http://jalonvalleyhelp.com

MURCIA MAR MENOR HELP

http://helpmurciamarmenor.org

VEGA BAJA HELP

http://helpvegabaja.com

And that, I am afraid, is largely it for free assistance. If you are registered on the Padron, and have your Residencia, you may find you can prise some home help out of your local Ayuntamento - but it´s not guaranteed. Most "at home" care in Spain is undertaken by the family, to a far greater extent than is usual in the UK. If you need ongoing medical care after hospitalization, you can most definitely expect regular visits at home from the Spanish equivalent of the District Nurse. They will provide palliative care for, say cancer treatment, and if you cannot get to your local Health Center will help with areas such as dressing changes. If you can manage to get to the Health Center, be warned! You will be expected to make the journey.

If you need more than a helping hand at home and are considering the equivalent of sheltered accommodation, then generally you will have to pay for it. But often older people use these facilities not because they need medical supervision or cannot manage at home, but rather because the better organizations offer all the security and care an older person needs, together with a comforting sense of community. You pays your money and you takes your choice, which is why, whenever possible, I have given the current costs for these facilities.

There are "Retirement Resorts" as they are generally called scattered throughout the Costa Blanca. They vary enormously in size and facilities. Some are actually attached to private hospitals (such as **Sol Vida**, which has apartments in the grounds of the Acuario Hospital in Beniarbeig, Costa Blanca North or the Residencia attached to the **Polyclinic at Teulada,** Costa Blanca North. The later is much more like a traditional elderly persons "Home" as residents have their own room rather than an apartment, and generally need quite a lot of support) so you are guaranteed excellent medical presence on a 24 hour basis. Others are independent complexes, where all residents are over a certain age.

The lower age limit for residency in such a complex appears to be around 55, which is terrifying. Perhaps I should move into one now, and save time later?

Facilities appear to vary enormously; some offer 24-hour medical help, with a permanent doctor on site. Others have access to a doctor on demand. Some will do your laundry and help with housework. Some will even give you three meals a day, included in your rental costs. Most have a restaurant, library, pool and sports facilities on site. Some are so vast and well appointed that you need never step off the complex, except to do a little shopping.

How you pay also varies greatly. Some apartments are purchased outright, and are yours to do with as you wish. Others are rented. At least one offers a lifetime-purchase option, where you pay a one-off lump sum.

I have researched as many as I could find information for. However, this is by no means a comprehensive list; there will be many more out there that either do not advertise because they are full, or find their residents by word of mouth. If you think you may need this sort of accommodation at some time in the future, I suggest you take a look at what is available in your area. As always, I cannot emphasise strongly enough that I am not recommending any of them, nor have I investigated any of the claims that they make. This chapter is purely for reference, to give you a flavour of what is available and what you can expect to pay. If you want to explore any of them further, please ensure that you make all your own enquiries. And please! Don´t complain about the grammar; it´s not mine, it´s the verbatim wording of the information supplied by the various companies.

To look at a few:

❖ **Retirement Resorts**

KEI Homes have a selection of retirement villages sprinkled throughout the Costa Blanca and beyond, including:

Colina Club, Calpe

"Colina Club Village comprises 48 one and two bedroom apartments on two levels, and a home that accommodates 20 private rooms. Connected to the rest home is the community room which offers a dining room/bar, extensive library and a large screen TV. The Colina Club Village is an English speaking adult community for the over 50´s. The Rest Home is situated in the exclusive 'Colina del Sol' urbanization, located in the countryside above Calpe. It offers a calm, quiet and restful family atmosphere - perfect for those who are looking for a place to relax and recuperate."

Facilities

- 24 hour nursing assistance/24hr emergency care (plus off and onsite care support)/24Hr Security/ Hospital close by/

Medical supervision if required/ Onsite Physiotherapist and Social Worker

- Bowling green -free to residents/ Golfing nearby/ Large Swimming pool - specifically designed for people with mobility difficulties
- Fresh nutritional home cooked menu
- HD TV and fast internet/WiFi/ Library/Large lounge area
- Mini bus service available for trips into town, the beach or excursions
- Private hourly, daily or live-in care assistance available
- Private parking/Short drive to the beach/Short drive to the town

Purchase Options

Short term rentals from one week to quarterly and long term rentals yearly.

Short term rentals in 1 bed apartment (1-3 Months) start from:

1. 250€ per week
2. 800€ per month
3. 1,800€ to 2,500€ per quarter

Long term rentals (6-12 Months) offer two options:

Gold Package (without medical and other services) starts from:

1. 450€ per month for 1 bedroom lower floor
2. 550€ for two bedroom, lower floor

Premium Package (which includes everything except electric) starts from:

1. 925€ per month for 1 bedroom lower floor
2. 975€ for one bedroom upper floor
3. 1,025€ for 2 bedroom lower floor
4. 1,100€ for 2 bedroom upper floor

Care home room costs start from 525€ per person/per week single and 900€ per couple/per week all inclusive

Cuidad Patricia, Benidorm

"Spacious single and double rooms, all with mountain views, adapted furniture, cable TV including international channels, air-conditioning/heating, WIFI, etc…

The building also has a hairdressing salon, podiatry, hot tubs, Jacuzzi, library, indoor and outdoor pool, central alarm, gym, solarium, some extensive terraces where you can enjoy the panoramic view that goes from Benidorm to Altea, and a cozy Mediterranean restaurant.

Registered nurses (on duty) 24 hours.

Our team provides a high level of care, the most suitable to enhance, maintain and restore the well-being of our residents, and thanks to the thorough work together with the doctor and our extensive experience in all types of nursing techniques, we avoid unnecessary hospital admissions.

Being as linked to our residents department, we believe it is necessary that the profile of our nurses be bilingual we deal with 8 different nationalities, the most important being Spanish and Dutch.*

Our most important techniques:

- Intravenous treatments and invasive techniques.
- Realization of soundings and stenting.
- Stitches and cures.
- Specific care of stoma.
- Blood samples either capillary or intravenous.
- Electrocardiographs.
- Palliative treatments.

Buy the lifelong right to live in the apartment. You don't have to worry about the increasing rent and the price is considerably lower than when you should buy a apartment. You don't have to pay conveyance tax.

The price depends on your age and the choice of your apartment. Our price list is based on 65 year-old persons. For each year that you are older we give you a discount of € 3.500, - and for each year you are younger you have to pay an extra of € 3.500. The average price for a 85 m2 apartment is € 140.000 for a 65 years-old person. When you are 75 years old you pay an average of € 105.000. In case two persons live in an apartment, the age of the youngest will be the base to calculate the price of the lifetime right of use.

You are free to end the contract at any time. There is a table for refunds for repayment in case you end early your contract.

There are monthly expenses of 274€. This service cost include...

- Building maintenance/Park maintenance/ Swimming pool maintenance/ Costs of use for the main central building
- Technical services, problem solving
- Care takers/Security
- Building insurance
- Refuse disposal
- TV channels
- Water consumption
- Organization of activities
- Shuttle service
- 24 hours medical emergency assistance/ GP visits during normal hours

The monthly service cost does not include electricity, telephone, internet and property tax (IBI) for individual apartments.

* Extremely unfortunate that the paragraph referring to the multi-lingual staff is in such fractured English! Or is it just me that's being ultra-picky?

Bon Retir, Javea

"Bon Retir Residential and Respite Care Home is situated in Javea on the Costa Blanca and provides dedicated residential and respite care to its residents, who are in need of either full time care or respite services in a warm family run Care Home.

Bon Retir Residential and Respite Care Home Javea, has been providing Residential and Respite Care Services to its clients in Javea and the Costa Blanca for more than 8 years and prides itself on the family orientated approach to the Care of your Loved ones.

Bon Retir Residential and Respite Care Home Javea, has all the facilities to care for your loved one on a short, medium or long term basis.

In Bon Retir Residential Care Home there is always a professional to take care of your loved ones, with kind attention and always available to help them in any situation. Our highly qualified staff composed of a doctor, nurse, clinical assistants, physiotherapist, psychologist, occupational therapist, social worker and other professionals as required, will guide you and your relative in the process of settling in our Home.

Our services: care and assistance: Keeping the body active is an important part of the quality of life that we want to provide to our residents. Our physiotherapist will study every case separately to give the best individual attention.

Our Target: make our residents feel at Home

Bon Retir has 20 private bedrooms, of which 10 are double and 10 single rooms. All bedrooms have the following facilities:

En suite toilet, with an adapted wet room/TV/Telephone/ Central heating/Alarm System in both bedroom and bathroom/Natural lighting with security windows and fly screens/An option of a terrace on ground floor rooms

The center has 2 large communal living rooms, with comfortable lounge seats to relax in, one with British TV. In Residencial Bon Retir you can enjoy bingo evenings, live entertainment, comedians and singers. In our Recreation Room you can select a book from our extensive library, or you can email your loved ones by using the internet or play one of the many games that are available. Bon Retir has a fully equipped kitchen with multilingual staff that also provides a mixed British and Spanish homemade cuisine. All menus are approved by our in-house Doctor. In addition, Bon Retir has a large patio area to walk and relax in, so you can enjoy the climate of the local area. We additionally have a small and cozy terrace and also a sun roof terrace.

Also provided are Doctor's surgery; hairdresser and chiropodist service; Laundry room; Physiotherapy room; Coffee and tea club.

Information in English:

Tel. 0034 688883155

Benimeli Residential, Northern Costa Blanca

"Our wide range of services include: Doctor's Surgery, Physiotherapy, Chiropody, Hairdresser, Laundry, Kitchen and Coffee Shop

The Center has 49 double bedrooms and two singles. If you wish, there's a possibility to convert a double room into a single, paying an extra charge. The bedroom prices are from 1.483 € monthly per bed (fortnightly stays are also possible). This price includes: meals, doctor, physiotherapy, occupational therapy, the gym and pool, and laundry services. We can arrange financing if required.

All the bedrooms have the following facilities: Air Conditioning, Central heating, Radiant Floor Heating, Telephone, TV connection, Direct bell to the infirmary in rooms and bathrooms, Wooden Floor, Desk, Piped Music, Adapted bathroom without architectural barriers, Elegant decoration.

And many, many more throughout the Costa Blanca North and South

If you do have the misfortune to have any unhappy experiences with any of the organizations I have mentioned, or for that matter any that I have not had space to mention I would be very grateful if you could take five minutes to drop me an e-mail and tell me about it. If this happens, I will be only too pleased to add a note describing the problems encountered, hopefully to stop anybody else experiencing it.

Chapter 6

Driving in Spain

I covered driving in Spain at length in Volume 1 of this series. However, in common with a surprising amount of tax legislation (see later) driving issues have also changed. So, in no particular order are the main areas you need to note:

❖ **Changing Your UK Driving Licence for a Spanish Licence**

Tráfico have finally, at long last, made up their minds about when you need to change your UK Driving Licence for a Spanish licence. This, after literally years, of issuing misinformation which has changed apparently monthly. As of April 2015, the situation is now:

According to Tráfico, anybody who is swapping a UK licence for a Spanish licence is not actually changing the licence, but is renewing it. Please note that the new legislation **only** applies to Residents, so if you are in possession of a Residencia, and live here for more than 183 days per year, this means you!

Tráfico´s official statement says:

"In order to clarify some of the confusion which has arisen over foreign residents in Spain changing their Driving Licence for a Spanish one, we have issued an instruction which details the obligations of both drivers and Law Enforcers in dealing with the issue.

Firstly, if your licence has an indefinite date, or more than 15 years validity (as was the   case with my own licence, which - shame on me! - was one of the old paper type) if you were legally resident in Spain before January 19th 2013, you should already have renewed your Driving Licence (i.e. you should have exchanged it for a Spanish licence. If you became resident after this date, you have up to 2 years from the date of becoming resident to renew.

Secondly, if your licence has expired or is due to expire; you must renew it in your country of residence. If you are resident in Spain, your current licence (no matter if it is from the UK, Ireland or (elsewhere) in the EU, once it expires, must be renewed in Spain."

Got that? In essence, get it changed or suffer the consequences. The good news is that you have a breathing space to get your licence in order, if needed. Tráfico have stated that no "sanctions or fines" will be applied before 1 January 2016, in order to assist residents in exchanging their licence for a Spanish one. The bad news? If you are stopped by the Guardia or police, and your licence is found to be faulty, then your details will be passed to the DGT. If you are stopped again, and your licence is still incorrect, then you will be fined €200.

Your new licence will expire at the same expiry date on your UK licence.

There is also a slightly annoying knock-on effect from this. When you change your UK licence for a Spanish one, you now have no option regarding the Medical. You **must** take a medical, as a new licence will not be issued unless you present your Medical Certificate on application.

I can tell you exactly what is involved, as my husband has just bitten the bullet (July 2015) and decided to change his licence. He was relieved to find that the Medical is ridiculously easy; it now consists of an eye test and a blood pressure reading and a couple of medical questions. In his case, the questions were: Do you wear glasses always? And what medication do you take? I should add that my husband is an insulin-dependant diabetic, so we were fully expecting to be asked to produce a report from our own doctor. This did not happen; the doctor simply asked if he had ever been hospitalized as a result of his diabetes, and when we said "no", that was that. And - to my mind oddly - we were asked what our average mileage per day was. No further questions! And don't worry - I don't know anybody who has managed to fail the Medical. A very dear friend in her eighties who took the test recently was so nervous she could barely see the eye test chart, and her blood pressure was through the roof for the same reason, but she still passed!

Most small towns have a test center, which rarely want an appointment - just check when they are open and turn up. They are often located in the same building as driving schools. Some private hospitals and clinics are also offering the test, but here you do need an appointment. You will find out when you make the appointment whether any English is spoken, if it isn't, it's well worth taking a translator with you. I did it for my husband, otherwise he would probably still have been there now....

The cost as at July 2015 (including IVA) is €44.80 for the medical. This includes taking a photograph for your Test Result Form, which you will need to submit to Alicante with your old licence (both parts), completed application form, Padron, Residencia and copy of your passport - all the usual suspects.

And a word of warning regarding the photographs for your licence. Wherever you take your medical they will generally take your photograph for your medical certificate, but not for your licence application - for that, you need another two photographs. You can use the photo booths in shopping centers, etc but take no notice whatsoever of the claim on the outside of the booth that the photograph is legal for all Spanish requirements. For the purposes of your licence application the photographs provided will be too big! You can either visit a professional photographer and ask for photographs "para conductor el coche", or you can - very, very carefully - cut down the booth photographs, ensuring that your full head and shoulders are clearly visible. The size needed is a tiny 26cm x 32 cms.

❖ What Documents Must I Keep in the Car?

Again, a few changes here. It used to be compulsory to have a record (bank statement, generally) of payment of your insurance premium, but this requirement has now gone.

You must still carry with you:

ITV Card

ITV Certificate (for cars more than 4 years old)

Permiso de Circulation (this is the document that gives details such as your registration number)
Insurance policy

Also advised to carry with you is your European Accident Agreement, which you are never going to need unless you have an accident, in which case it is very useful - ask your insurer for a version in English.

And ... apart from your insurance details, for which a copy is fine, you need to have in the car either originals, or copies that have been certified by a Notary.

❖ **How do I Replace Lost or Stolen Documents for my Vehicle?**

For once, it´s reasonably easy!

The advice is **always** to report lost or stolen vehicle documents to your nearest Policia Local. If you don´t do this, you run the risk of accumulating fines if somebody misuses your vehicle, and it´s possible someone may use your documents for identity fraud.

Once you have reported the loss to the Policia Local (and obtained a report):

a)   Make an appointment in the Traffic Office (in Alicante - sorry, you have to do this in person, and I strongly suggest taking an Interpreter with you) by calling 060. Obviously, you need as many details of your car as you can remember, and - as usual - it´s not going to hurt to take at least your passport with you, and if possible your copy of the Padron and your Residencia. You may not be asked for them, but if you are, it´s a lot easier to have them to hand than to have to make a return trip to Alicante! I actually scan all my vehicle documents on a "just in case" basis.

b) Alicante will then issue a new Logbook / Driving Licence, as appropriate. This is yet another reason to get a Spanish Driving Licence!

c) If your vehicle has already had an ITV, you will have to visit the local ITV Station and explain the situation to the person behind the front desk. If you take all your documents with you, this shouldn't be a problem. They will then issue with a duplicate ITV certificate.

❖ Child Safety in Vehicles

Be warned; the police are quite fierce about child safety in cars. The rules are
size rather than age based. Until children are 1.35 meters in height they must use a "restraint seat" (baby seat, booster etc) Between 1.35 m and 1.50 m height you can choose what to use as long as the child is safely restricted. From 1.50m in height they have to use only the seat belt.

❖ Seat Belts and Dog Safety

Worth pointing out that if you are in a moving vehicle, you **must** wear a seat belt at all times. This applies to van delivery drivers, normal drivers, passengers, coach couriers etc you will get fined if they catch you without one. Even your dog must be secured, either to a seat belt point, a fixed point in the rear of the car or be travelling behind a secure dog guard. This, of course, does not explain why I saw a completely unsecured dog travelling in a totally open sided beach buggy being driven at speed down the N332 yesterday. Mind you, this uber-cool pooch was actually wearing sun-glasses so if Tráfico stopped the owner they would probably have been too busy laughing to actually give him a fine.

❖ Towing

And just a final word regarding towing cars ....Don´t do it! Even if you have broken down, don´t ask a friend to tow you to the nearest garage, using a tow bar or rope. The only way that a car can be towed legally in this way in Spain is by a "Grua"; a specialised tow truck. You may wish to note that this prohibition also applies to cars towed by Motor Homes; it´s still illegal, and if the Guardia or Police spot you, you will be fined and your vehicle could be immobilized. In order to tow legally, your vehicle must have a proper A-bar attachment fitted; a normal tow bar attachment is simply not enough.

Chapter 7

Passports - Renewing and Losing

Just because you have elected to live in Spain it does not deprive you of your British - or any other country's - passport. It is still valid for the same length of time, and you still have to renew it, and pay for that renewal. It´s just the method of obtaining it that differs to renewing in the UK.

I am assuming that since you have found your way here, you already have a passport, so will need to renew it eventually. And I do apologise for those readers who are from outside the UK; as processes differ so widely from country to country, I am only dealing here with the process as applicable to UK nationals.

The UK process of renewal has changed in recent years, and at present if you are resident in Spain it can **only be done on line**. These are the instructions for renewing a standard, adult passport.

The good news? It costs less this year than it did last year!

Full instructions for renewal are given on **https://www.gov.uk/overseas-passports/y/spain/renewing_new/adult.**

❖ You should note that your application will take **at least** 6 weeks. That's six weeks from when it´s received by the Passport Office in the UK; **not** 6 weeks from when you applied. The six week period will take longer if you do not send all the required documents, or your photographs don´t meet the Passport Offices requirements (See below for more on photographs):

❖ The Passport Office may ask you attend an interview prior to issuing your new passport; there is no reason given as to why this might arise, or what circumstances will trigger an interview. If it happens to you, I strongly advise you to ask what the problem is before booking your flight back to the UK.

❖ The cost of your passport is divided into 2; a courier fee of £19.86 and a passport fee of £83 for a standard 32 page passport. If you want a 48 page passport, the fee is £91. If you were born before 1929, your passport is free of cost.

❖   To apply for your passport, you will need:

1. Your old passport

2. Two identical photographs of yourself. Be warned! The Passport Office is very fussy about what it will accept in the way of photographs. Your face cannot be obscured in any way, nor can you be smiling in the photograph. Not only must the photographs be a standard size, it is also essential that your face is correctly displayed in the photograph - e.g. there must only be a certain amount of space above your head. You can get passport photographs from booths in Spain, but from experience I can state that it takes a great deal of seat-adjusting and slouching to get it right - not to mention several attempts. Much easier to find a local photographic shop - anywhere that does family photographs will be set up to take them for you, just be sure to mention that it is for a British passport photograph. Cost is around €6 - €8, depending on how posh your

photographer is. And you can easily spend that on multiple attempts in a booth!

3. A valid credit or debit card number is needed for payment. Spanish MasterCard, Visa, Visa Electron, Visa Debit are accepted, as are Maestro (UK Domestic) cards. Spanish or other international Maestro cards are **not** accepted

4. Remember to get your application countersigned. This has to be by a professional person (including those who are retired) for example, bank or building-society officials, police officers, civil servants, ministers of religion and people with professional qualifications like teachers, accountants, engineers and solicitors – you can find a full list at www.gov.uk/ countersigning-passport-applications. The person has to have known you for at least 2 years, and hold a British, Irish, EU or US

current passport. Relatives are not allowed to countersign.

5. Even though you are applying on line, you will still need to print off your application to enable you to sign the declaration form at the end. Nor can you then scan your application and submit it electronically - the hard copy application form and all supporting documents have to be posted in hard copy to the passport office in the UK.

6. You will need to complete your contact details on the form. Always give a current telephone number where you can be reached - the courier will ring when they are ready to arrive.

All of this is fine if you have plenty of time to apply for your new passport. But **what if your passport has been lost or stolen,** and you want to travel soon after the loss? Be warned, you are unlikely to be allowed to apply for an emergency passport if you are travelling more than 5 days after you discover the loss. In this case, you will be expected to get a full, new passport.

The first thing to note is that it's an expensive business! An emergency passport (which still has to be exchanged for a full passport and will only allow you one overseas journey, and back again if you are resident in Spain) is going to cost you £95 (or the going rate equivalent in euros. Ouch!) You can apply for what is called "an emergency travel document" (an emergency passport by any other name) if you are a British national outside the UK and your passport has been lost, stolen or damaged. If it has been stolen, it is also an excellent idea to report the theft to your local police station. If you require an emergency passport, this is vital; the British Consulate will require a police report before issuing your emergency passport. I strongly advise either having a copy of your passport reduced and laminated, and/or taking a copy or scan of it yourself. Either way, if it is lost, it's so much easier to be able to have all the details to hand.

And even worse news - you must apply in person. On the Costa Blanca, the nearest Consulate is in Alicante. You must take with you:

- ❖ a completed application form for an emergency passport (available to download at https://www.gov.uk/government/publications/application-for-a-united-kingdom-emergency-travel-document.
- ❖ a recent passport-quality photo (and if you are using a machine, check that it is valid for a UK passport)

❖ proof of your travel plans, e.g. booking confirmations (or detailed written travel plans if you can't book ahead)

❖ A police report if your passport has been stolen.

The Consulate will not guarantee that you will get your emergency passport the same day, although they will do their best if all your supporting documentation is in order and your travel plans are straightforward.

Chapter 8

Non Resident Tax Issues

I know, this Guide is supposed to be for those sensible people who want to relocate here permanently. But I have had a lot of questions from people who fully expect to retire here eventually, but not just yet. They have bought property, but it may be two, three or more years before they can wave good-bye to paid employment and retire to the sun, in peace. So, this chapter is for those of you who have bought property on the Costa Blanca - or are intending to do so - and need to know the basic rules and regulations that apply whilst you are still legally an absentee landlord.

To begin with, if you intend to spend some time in Spain, and some time in the UK (or elsewhere) for a time, how do you decide if you are resident here or not?

The English Taxman has a whole raft of areas he wants to consider. Here in Spain, the test is much simpler. **If you live in Spain for more than 183 days a year then you are a resident**

here. Simple as that. Just one day less, and you are officially non-resident. And by the way, that is not necessarily consecutive days - it is 183 days in any one year, no matter how widely spaced those days are.

Unfortunately, the fact that you are officially non-resident doesn't mean that you don't have to conform to Spanish rules and regulations. You do, and you also have to pay certain property taxes, just the same as those of who are resident.

These are:

- ❖ **IBI** (Impuesto Sobre Bienes Inmuebles) - this is basically the Spanish equivalent of Council Tax. It is based on the value of the land your property stands on (and is payable for all types of inhabitable property, from luxurious villas to the tiniest of studio apartments). This is payable by anybody who owns property in Spain, and is calculated in exactly the same way, no matter if you are resident or non-resident.

  IBI is paid directly to your local Council, either on demand by them or via the collection agency (SUMA). It is paid annually, but at different times depending on your Council. Best way to pay it is to set up a standing order at your bank;

you may still get a written reminder, but ignore it (apart from checking that your standing order has been paid).

❖ If you are non-resident and own property here, you also have to pay what is called **"imputed income tax" and/or rental tax** (in some cases, you may be clobbered with a combination of the two).

Imputed Income Tax is generally viewed as the most unfair tax ever dreamed up by anybody, anywhere. You have no choice as to whether you pay it or not. Even if the principles behind it do not apply to you, you must still pay it.

To put it at its simplest, if you are non-resident and own a property in Spain, then the Government simply assumes that you are going to rent it out, whether you do or not. This leads to not one, but two, tax "opportunities".

1) If you never rent out your Spanish property, and have no intention of ever doing so, the Government still takes the view that you *could* rent it out, if you wanted to. In this case, you will pay "imputed income tax" on the property. I know, it´s grossly unfair, but at present it´s regarded as a legitimate tax, and cannot be avoided.

Your Spanish property has to be declared on the annual non-resident annual tax declaration (see below for details) and whatever amount the Hacienda (the Spanish Taxman) comes up with, you will be expected to pay.

2) If you **do** rent out your property (or if you are prepared to admit to the Hacienda that you do so, not quite the same thing!) then you will need to pay, in addition to imputed income tax, **rental tax** on your Spanish property.

This is collected quarterly on:

20th April

20th July

20th October

20th January

How much you pay is based on the rental income that you declare; the tax is payable on the gross amount you declare, and makes no allowances for costs such as cleaning, pool care, maintenance, etc. And beware; the Hacienda may not be very good at telling you about your tax liabilities, but they are excellent at demanding anything that is owed!

❖ Moving on to the **paperwork**. As a New Year present, if you are non-resident you **must** make your **annual non-resident tax declaration** no later than 31st December every year.

The declaration is retrospective (it covers the previous year) and is the basis of deciding how much tax you owe either for **imputed income tax or rental tax**.

In the past, many non-resident owners risked getting away without making the declaration, on the basis that they were in England and nothing happens quickly in Spain, and anyway, how is the Hacienda going to track me down in England? Now, this is really, really not a good idea. The Hacienda has become increasingly efficient in recent years, and is now keen on areas such as checking with the Land Registry to see who owns which property, and monitoring electric consumption. You may get away with it, but if you don't, the penalties are extremely unpleasant.

If you either don't make your annual declaration, or don't pay your taxes, then the following list of "nasties" may come into force:

1. The tax debt is held against your property until it is either sold or bequeathed. It is then payable - with interest, of course.

2. If you want to sell, you cannot change the names on the Title Deed until the debt is settled.

3. Your bank account can be embargoed, i.e. it is frozen so that no money can go in or out. You then find you cannot pay your utility bills or anything else, so the debts mount up even more.

And you can´t rely on the Hacienda (the Spanish Tax Office) chasing you to make any outstanding submissions. They *may* send you a warning letter, assuming they find out you are in arrears, but it´s not guaranteed. They don´t have to! Also, of course, as you are in the UK for most of the year, you may not even receive it. The letter - if any - will be sent to your Spanish address. If you are not there to receive it, it will be returned to the Correos, who will leave you a Notification Form to say you have X days in which to collect (normally no more than fifteen, often seven - depends on the categorization of the letter). If you do not collect it within the given period, Correos will simply return it to the Hacienda as "undelivered". In this case, Hacienda will consider that their duty has been done, and if you fail to respond, the list given above may well come into force. The first you are likely to know about it is when your bank account is frozen.

The easiest way to stop this happening is to do it right in the first place; make your annual declaration and *then* grumble about the tax. I would strongly recommend getting yourself a decent Spanish accountant. They will ensure that your return is made on time, and can also set up all your standing orders for you. A decent accountant will always be happy to give you free advice about tax matters and "how it´s done" for anything financial. There are dozens of them out there, and many of them are now happy to work with you via e-mail; very useful when you are not here. We have had an accountant from the day we bought our property here. The current fee is €100 + Iva per year, and even though I now live here full time, I would never do without my accountant.

Chapter 9

Working in Spain

Hoping to get a job when you move across? A few years ago, it would have been easily achievable. In the boom days of the construction wave, bars, restaurants and shops were only too happy to employ native English speakers.

Now, however, times are hard. Spain has an unemployment rate of around 25%; many younger people have never worked at all, and are dependant on their families for food and lodging. It´s worth noting that the benefit system here in Spain is nowhere near as generous as it is in the UK. You do not qualify for any sort of State benefit whatsoever unless you have paid into the system. If you have worked over here, and paid your taxes and Social Security, you may qualify for some benefits, but these are based on both the amount you were earning and the length of time you were employed. Even if you are eligible for some benefits, when they expire, that's it. There are no supplemental payments in force, as in the UK.

Having said that, there are signs that the economy is picking up. More property is selling, and there is even new build taking place again. At least in the holiday season, bars and restaurants are bustling.

Your chance of getting paid employment will vary greatly depending on where you live, and your language skills. If you live on the coast - or are prepared to commute - then you may be able to get a job in a local bar, particularly in the tourist resorts. Even here, at least some basic Spanish is generally required.

If you are multilingual, and in particular speak German as well as basic Spanish and (of course!) good English, the market is wider. As more property begins to sell, Estate Agents and what are ubiquitously titled "wealth management" companies (basically, investment advisors) are beginning to advertise for staff. Some call centers are also beginning to advertise for staff, as are funeral plan retailers. But beware; both call centers and funeral plan retailers tend to pay purely on a commission basis, so no sales, no salary. If you have to travel to meet clients, then check that they will pay expenses, or otherwise you could not only end up working for nothing, but actually be out of pocket if no expenses are paid.

In the event that you are lucky enough to get a job offer, check that it comes with a contract. This will cover what you are paid and what hours you are to work. Even more importantly, a job with a contract - no matter how meager the wages - entitles you to State health care whilst you are employed. You will also pay tax, and National Insurance which will qualify you for benefits (at least for some time) if you become unemployed, and will also count towards a Spanish pension. A job where money is paid "into your hand" is not only illegal; it means you get no benefits whatsoever. It also stands a good chance of landing you in trouble with the authorities. Because unemployment is so high in Spain, checks are made regularly on the normal suspects (particularly bars and restaurants and construction sites) and you are likely to be asked to provide proof that your employment is official.

It's quite likely that you may never have heard of **Beckham's Law**. Learn to love it, it could be advantageous to you! Football fan or not, if you are employed on a contract as an employee of a Spanish enterprise and are earning a great deal of money (up to €600,000 per year! I wish…), you may well have a great deal to thank David Beckham for. It's unlikely to apply to that many of us, but I mention it here out of interest.

It works like this:

You have to be a non-Spanish national, who lives and works in Spain. If you are, you can elect to pay income tax as if you were non-resident for up to the first 5 years you are fiscally resident here. Now why would you want to do that? Two reasons:

1. The non-resident rate of tax is a flat 24.75% of income. Residents, on the other hand, pay around 22% at the basic rate, **rising to 52% at the higher tax bands**.
2. Residents are taxed on worldwide income, but under Beckham's Law you only have to pay tax in Spain on the money you earn in Spain.

So you are no doubt asking yourself why anybody who pays more than the basic rate of tax isn't taking advantage of this scheme? The main reason is that although the non-resident tax rate is lower, you do not get any personal allowances, which - unless you are earning a very large amount of money indeed - is likely to mean it is not worthwhile.

And don't forget, unless you have an amazingly good accountant it's more than likely that the portion of income that is not taxed in Spain will be taxed somewhere in the world. So unless you have a fiscal hideout somewhere very, very advantageous, you may not be that well off in the long run. Apparently Mr. Beckham made this work to his advantage, but then again, you may well not be earning as much as he did.

If you want to work in a **self-employed capacity**, assuming you have the customers there is nothing at all to stop you. Many people pick up an extra bit of money by cleaning villas and pools locally, or doing odd jobs for friends and neighbours. A certain amount of this kind of thing may be tolerated, but if you intend earning your living in this way, you should be registered as self-employed. And a word of warning; do not try and set yourself up as a taxi service, particularly for airport runs. Every time you park in the airport carport, even if it is only for half an hour, a photograph of your number plate is taken. If you car is seen coming and going frequently, you will be suspected of running an illegal taxi service. This is frowned upon by the authorities, and you are more than likely to get a visit from the Guardia, together with a slapped wrist and the strong possibility of a hefty fine.

Before you do decide to start up a business on your own here in the lovely Costa Blanca, it really is a good idea to do it right and get the paperwork sorted. The main area to be aware of is it the "**Autonomo**" system.

The Autonomo system applies to all self-employed people, and encompasses the spectrum from self-employed builders to shop and bar owners' right through to independent doctors, accountants and professional people generally. Very, very basically it is the equivalent of the national insurance payments made by those who are self-employed in the UK

The bare outlines are as follows, but please note! These are just guidelines, designed to give you no more than a flavour of what you need to do to become legally self employed in Spain. If you really are keen to give it a go, you **must** get an Abogado and get professional legal advice.

And - although this is not actually set out in black and white anywhere that I can find - it appears unlikely that the tax man is going to demand that you go on the Autonomo if you are earning only a small amount, at irregular intervals. But if in doubt, check! The only actual figure I can find anywhere is that if you earn above the official yearly minimum wage working on a self-employed basis, you must pay the Autonomo - at present, this amount is €9,080 per annum.

❖ **Categories of Self-Employed "Traders" Captured by the Autonomo**

The full list is almost endless, and each category has a huge number of sub-divisions. Whatever you want to do, it has to be in here somewhere! I have given only the main headings, as - for instance - the category of "Agriculture, Forestry and Fishing" includes such diverse areas as "growing of non-perennial crops", "raising of cattle and buffaloes" and "gathering of wild-growing non-wood products".

These are the basic "Autonomo" categories:

AGRICULTURE, FORESTRY AND FISHING
MINING AND QUARRYING
MANUFACTURING (Includes repairs and installation)
ELECTRICITY, GAS, STEAM AND AIR CONDITIONING
SUPPLY WHOLESALE AND RETAIL TRADE
REPAIR OF MOTOR VEHICLES / AND MOTORCYCLES
INFORMATION AND COMMUNICATION
PUBLIC ADMINISTRATION AND DEFENCE
COMPULSORY SOCIAL SECURITY
EDUCATION
HUMAN HEALTH AND SOCIAL WORK ACTIVITIES
ARTS, ENTERTAINMENT AND RECREATION
OTHER SERVICE ACTIVITIES
ACTIVITIES OF HOUSEHOLDS AS EMPLOYERS
UNDIFFERENTIATED GOODS - AND SERVICES
PRODUCING ACTIVITIES OF HOUSEHOLDS FOR OWN
USE
ACTIVITIES OF EXTRATERRITORIAL ORGANIZATIONS
AND BODIES

Phew! Enough choice there for you? Literally something for everyone! And - believe it or not - joining the Autonomo system is the quickest and easiest way to become self-employed in Spain, and it is certainly the option most people go for.

❖ **Advantages of the Autonomo**

1. These are basically as I set out above. You are fully legal - no chance of the Guardia knocking on your door and closing you down. And yes, it does happen. I visited a craft shop recently that I have used for some

months, to find it was having a "closing down sale". When I asked why, I was told that the woman who ran the shop had no idea that she should have been registered for Autonomo, and had no intention of doing so. As a result, the authorities had told her she must register or close.

2. You also **qualify for State health care, for both you and your family**, and can build up some credits towards other benefits.

❖ **Disadvantages of the Autonomo**

Basically, it boils down to two main points.

1. Firstly, there is the nuisance element of having to do it. Easiest way is to get an accountant or legal representative to do all the registration elements for you, but of course they will charge you for this.

2. The other point is the cost, which is impressively large. At the time of writing (April 2015) the normal "Autonomo" cost is a hefty €264 **per month**, which is payable for each month you are working on a self-employed basis. If you are over 50, add on another €20. It is payable monthly, so if you are not earning

anything one month, you simply don´t go to the bank
and pay it that month.

There are schemes (mainly for new start ups) that offer
reductions in the payment amount for certain periods. And if you
are a market trader (officially categorized as a "peddler"!) you will
pay less.

This barely scratches the surface of the Autonomo scheme: it is
large, complex and - to any non-accountant - thoroughly
bewildering. Some exemptions are available, but there are also
provisions for the demand for Iva (VAT) returns, invoicing, etc. All
I can hope to do here is make you aware of it, if you think you may
be liable for Autonomo, please, get professional assistance.

Chapter 10

Buying Property at Auction - If You Really Must

If you really want to buy property at auction in Spain, on your own head be it!

I did say in Volume 1 that I would never, ever recommend buying property at auction in Spain. The procedure is both different to how it works in the UK, and - given the fact that you have the language barrier and Spanish law also takes a different approach to what you are used to - far more complex. However, I have had a number of requests for clarification on the legal process, so here goes!

Firstly, it should be said that it is perfectly possible to snap up a bargain at auction. Property sold in this way is normally bank repossessions. In these circumstances, the bank or mortgage company is basically only interested in clearing their outstanding debt amount, so property is unlikely to achieve market value.

But if you must do it, take care! The following is the absolute basics of how it works in Spain.

❖ **The Legal background**.

Contrary to what many people believe, auctions in Spain **are** regulated by the Courts - to be precise, by the Spanish Civil Proceedings laws - to a far greater degree than is the case in the UK. The Courts actually set the price of the property to be auctioned, depending in part on the amount owing on the property. The way the auction works is also formalized by the court; in Spain, there are different scenarios depending on how high the "winning" bid is. Very generally, the highest bid will be sought at a level that is at least 70% of the court-decided price. If no bids are received above this level, you may think that yours was the winning bid, but it may still be unsuccessful as the sum bid is insufficient to cover the outstanding debt on the property. This is down to the authorities to decide. Told you it was complicated!

You must also be aware that if you do buy at auction, you will be then immediately be liable for any outstanding debts against the property, such as utility bills or unpaid community fees. And what you see is what you get! If the property is falling down, hard lines - you should have inspected it before you put a bid in. Once your bid is accepted, you cannot back out just because you are not happy with the deal. **There is no cooling off period when you can change**

your mind. And make sure you either have the full cash amount available, or guaranteed mortgage funding to hand.

And equally always make sure that you have an extra 10% of the purchase price in your pocket, as you will have to pay Property Transfer Tax, which in Valencia is 10% of the final acquisition price of the auction property.

And please, don´t just turn up on the day of the auction and expect to be allowed to bid. That is not going to happen! All of the auction organizations have their own procedures in place, and they are all likely to want to go through various financial checks beforehand, to ensure that you are not bidding with no intention of completing. At the very least, you have to register and fill in the inevitable forms in advance of the auction.

❖ **Useful Websites**

If you are still interested in giving it a go these are the official Spanish Government websites, together with a few official auctioneers. Some have English speaking contacts/websites, some do not. If you are really committed to buying at auction, I cannot suggest strongly enough that you get in touch with an Abogado (legal advisor) who specializes in this area, and who can talk you through the process and, preferably, go with you on the day. And - forgive me for telling my Granny how to suck eggs - if you are going to arrive in Spain with a pocket full of cash to buy at auction, don't tell the world (and especially not the nice chap you've just met who is standing next to you at the bar) about it.

There was a particularly nasty murder in Benidorm a couple of years ago, when a couple arrived from the UK and did just that, and were murdered by an man they were talking to in a bar for the auction money they were actually carrying about with them. And which they bragged about. Self-evidently not a good idea.

❖ **Auction Internet Sites**

http//:www.agenciatributaria.es/AEAT.internet/en_gb/Inicio_en_GB/La_Agencia_Tributaria/Subastas/Subastas.shtml – Site is in Spanish (updated now also in so-so English) but is fairly self explanatory. Lots of cheap auction properties held regularly which have arisen through non payment of taxes bank repossessions etc.

http://defensa.gob.es/ccfas/SUBASTAS - Direct property disposal and auctions, site is available in English.

http://invied.mde.es/en/index.html?_locale=en Property auctions and direct sales - site is available in English.

http://www.segsocial.es/Internet_1/Lanzadera/index.htm?MIval =cw_lanzadera&URL=4 - Lots of property in various areas for disposal, sometimes other items such as cars etc.

http:// orgt.diba.es/esp/O5venbie.asp Properties for disposal in and around Barcelona. Even though it´s out of the Costa Blanca, well worth a look for property in this most desirable of areas.

http://www.consorseguros.es/web/ad_al_vd_ps Property auctions together with other assets.

❖ **Other Property Auction Resources**

These are mainly private auction sites where an individual has submitted their property to a company for a quick sale, which is reflected in the price. As far as I am aware, these sites are reputable but please note they are **not** Government sites so if you want to bid with them, I strongly advise asking your Abogado for advice as to whether they are financially safe.

http://www.segipsa.es – Regular public auctions from private and government sources.

http://www.subastas.bnpparibas.es - Live auctions, downloadable auction catalogue

Well worth taking a look at some of these sites to see what is on offer out there, but if you are a first time purchaser on the Costa Blanca, I would still strongly advise against going down this route. It adds complexity and risk to what is already a fairly complex process.

Aside from auctions, if you are interested in "bargain" property, most of the local estate agents have a "bucket" list of properties for sale which residents are in a hurry to sell, often together with some bank repossessions. I would always go there first. In addition, some of the banks also offer their own repossession list; Sabadell is a good one to check out, as the site is available in excellent English and is easy to navigate.

In any event, good luck and take care!

Chapter 11

Can I get my Property Deposit Back?

The answer is …. yes and no. Come on, this is Spain! Did you really expect it to be straightforward?

To begin with the negative. Unlike the UK, there is no such a thing as a "cooling off" period after purchase. If you simply go away and realise that the dream villa you decided to put a deposit on is not, after all, for you, then if the reason you are withdrawing is simply because you have changed your mind, you cannot claim your deposit back. This applies even if you change your mind same day that the deposit is made - the seller has no legal obligation to give you your money back.

If, however, there is a legal reason for your change of heart (what is called in the UK "supervening illegality") then you **are** fully entitled to reclaim every penny of your deposit. The key here is the word "legal". You must have a valid legal reason for changing your mind. For instance, you discover that the property is not fully legal itself - e.g. it doesn't have a cedula, and the Vendor did not disclose this to you. Or if the Vendor has told you (preferably in writing) that the property is connected to the mains electric supply, and it is not. If there is either a legal error, or a demonstrable and important (I hesitate to use the word "blatant" but that is what it amounts to) aspect to the property which is not in accordance with what you were led to expect, then you can claim your deposit back.

If you are buying through a reputable estate agent, the process of claiming a deposit back should be easier. To take the example of no electricity connection again; if the estate agent has advertised the property as having all mains connections, then you have relied on the estate agent's description, which you have in writing somewhere - even if only on the internet advertisement. In this case, the Vendor cannot pretend to be innocent and claim that he had already mentioned the lack of electric to you. If you are dealing direct with the Vendor, then it is an excellent idea to make sure that all the details he has advertised are, in fact, correct before you make an offer. If they are not, and you are happy to accept the differences, use it as a bargaining point to get the price down. But don't forget, once accepted you cannot use the changes to back out of the deal.

But what if you have put a deposit on a property "off plan" and the Developer has gone bankrupt before your property has been constructed, with no bank guarantee in place? There is now a ray of hope! A few years ago, the answer would have been "hard lines". If your Developer had gone bankrupt, then you had no chance at all of getting your deposit back, or at best, not for years until the legal dust had settled.

New legislation has clarified this aspect, and it is most definitely in favour of you, the purchaser.

The law will now help you recover your deposit if your deposit was paid at any time **within the last fifteen years.** The relevant legislation is Law 57/68.

There are two scenarios where your deposit will be returned.

1. Firstly, your Developer should have taken out a bank guarantee or insurance guarantee in respect of your property. If he has, then you can claim your deposit back from the bank or insurance company holding the guarantee.

2. If the Developer has not taken out the relevant guarantees, in the past you were highly unlikely ever to see a penny of your deposit again. It is in these cases where the new legislation is extremely beneficial. In essence, the legislation states that **the bank** into which your Developer paid your deposit is now responsible for returning that deposit.

The relevant bank must take responsibility for returning your deposit in the following circumstances:

- ❖ The property is not complete and has not been handed over to you, and
- ❖ .The Developer has not taken out the prescribed guarantees.

In the case where the Developer has been naughty and not taken out the required guarantees, a Supreme Court judgement of January 2015 confirmed that even where there was never a bank guarantee in existence, then the Developer's bank is still responsible for returning your deposit. This judgement also confirmed the limitation period of 15 years from placing the deposit.

Obviously, if you find yourself in the situation of needing to claim under this legislation, you are going to need a legal representative. There are a number of Spanish companies (most of them also English speaking) who will be more than happy to undertake your claim for you - take a look in virtually any free paper to find them. Fortunately, the English idea of "no win - no fee" is now beginning to creep into Spain, and at least a couple of the companies who advertise in this area state that they are happy to pursue your claim in this way.

Chapter 12

Changes to Inheritence Tax Regulations for Non-Residents

A great deal of good news on this front, at least for those of you who either wish to simply keep a holiday home here on the Costa Blanca, or do not want to live here as a "tax resident". Or, of course, want to wait a few years before finally moving across. Although it doesn´t directly affect those of you who are longing to move here permanently, as soon as possible, it is still well worth mentioning for the many people who will get here eventually, but not just yet.

The Spanish tax regime for non-residents who died leaving property or assets in Spain was, until January of 2015, best described as grossly unfair. For non-residents who died leaving property or assets in Spain, especially where their heirs lived outside Spain, the tax regime was simple - you (or rather your inheritors) were liable for tax on the whole amount of the inheritence - there were no allowances whatsover. And the Taxman simply did not care whether your heirs intended to sell the assets or not; even if it was intended to keep them for their own use, they were taxed on their full value. This could mean that the Taxman claimed the greater part of any inheritence, and what's more, he wanted his money quickly - even if your heirs had to, say, sell property to meet the tax liability, the Taxman would not wait for the sale to go through before claiming his share. This applied even if you were leaving property to your husband/wife, and that property was owned in joint names. You were expected to pay within a few months, and if you did not, then interest was added to the sum owing originally.

Now, I am delighted to say, the European Court has very wisely decided that this is discriminatory to non-Spanish EU residents, and the Spanish Taxman has been told to mend his ways. As from January 2015, if you own assets or property in Spain, even if you are legally non-resident, then your **heirs will be taxed as if they are Spanish residents**. And a little icing on the cake as well; this is national law, but you will still be assesed for tax on a regional basis. For instance, if the deceased is an EU citizen with assets in Spain but was not resident at the time of death, you - as the legatee - can choose to be taxed under the law of the Autonomous Region where the assets are located. If the deceased was resident, then you can choose to be taxed under the law of his or her place of residence.

This may seem a complex irrelevance, but it is actually very important. Although Spain is is a country in the legal sense, it is really a collection of Autonomous Regions ("Comunidads Autónomas"). Each region is very much an entity in its own right, with a differing set of rules and regulations, and also differing tax regimes. Valencia - at least in respect of inheritance tax regulations - is relatively kind to its inhabitants and those who own property here.

The following charts and information (apologies for the apparent complexity, it does make sense if you read it through) sets out the allowances given to **both** Spanish and non-Spanish inheritors in Valencia.

The final column in the chart (highlighted in **bold**) shows the tax regime applicable to non-Spanish inheritors **prior to January 2015**. Except to take a deep breath of relief, ignore this column! If you are inheriting assets of any sort in Spain, no matter whether your benefactor was resident in Spain or not, and regardless of whether you are resident in Spain or not, if the assets are located in Valencia, or the person who has willed the assets to you was resident in Valencia, then the allowances given in the second column apply to you, and your wallet will be very grateful!

So, the nitty gritty of the new regime.

It´s worth pointing out that there is still a difference between fiscally resident and non-resident status when it comes to world-wide assets. This area has not been changed by the new legislation. If you are an ex-pat **fiscally resident** in Spain, then you are liable to pay Spanish Inheritance Tax **regardless of where the inheritance is actually situated** (i.e. you will be taxed on an inheritance in the UK, or anywhere else in the world, here in Spain). Fortunately, as a result of the double-taxation treaty with the UK, you will only be liable for tax in Spain, and not also in the UK. If you are **non-resident**, on death then you are liable to **pay Inheritance Tax only on assets actually located in Spain.**

For either Residents or non-Residents alike, there are 4 classes of "inheritors" with different allowances for each class. The figures given in brackets are the relevant allowances, correct as at 2015. These classes are:

Group 1: "Natural descendants" (children) and adopted children under age 21 at the time of the inheritance.

Group 2: Natural descendants and adopted children over 21 at the time of the inheritance, together with legal spouses, parents and adoptive parents

Group 3: Brothers/sisters, nephews/nieces, aunts/uncles

Group 4: Relatives in forth degree (e.g cousins) or friends (what are known in Spain as "non-blood"). (No allowances).

The reason for distinguishing between **Groups 1 and 2** is that there is a graduated threshold for **Spanish inheritance tax payments** for children and grandchildren under the age of 21. For every year that **each** child is under the age of 21 they receive an additional **€8,000 regardless of residence** up to a maximum allowance of **€47,858/ 96,000€ each respectively**.

Worth bearing in mind is the timescale for submission of Inheritance Tax demands. You have **6 months** in which to pay your tax. After this, it´s a fine for late payment of 5% for every 3 months overdue, up to a maximum of 20% extra.

All figures are accurate as at the time of writing.

Group	Resident/non-resident Applicable after January 2015	Non-Resident NOT APPLICABLE AFTER JANUARY 2015
1. Descendent below the age of 21 (includes children and grand-children)	**€40,000 for each child** with an additional €8,000 for every year they are under 21 to a maximum of **€96,000**	**€15,956.87 for each child with an additional €8,000 for every year they are under 21 to a maximum of €47,858**

2.Grand-children and children older than 21, parents, spouse	€40,000 each beneficiary	**€15,956 each beneficiary**
3. Sisters, brothers, aunts/ uncles, nephews / nieces and parents in law	€7,993 each	**€7,993 each**
4. Others (not "blood" relation	No allowance applies	**No allowance applies**

Once the allowances set out above have been deducted the Hacienda applies the following tax rates on the remainder of the inheritance, if any. These are now applicable to Resident and non-Resident alike:

AMOUNT	Percent (%)
0 up to 7,993.46€	7.65
Up to 15,980.91€	8.50
Up to 23,968.36€	9.35
Up to 31,955.81€	10.20
Up to 39,943.26€	11.05
Up to 47,930.72€	11.90
Up to 55,918.17€	12.75
Up to 63,905.62€	13.60
Up to 71,893.07€	14.45
Up to 79,880.52€	15.30

Up to 119,757.67€	16.15
Up to 159,634.83€	18.70
Up to 239,389.13€	21.25
Up to 397,55.08€	25.50
Up to 797,555.08€	29.75
Over 797,555.08€	34.00

You may well be thinking that the surviving spouse is fairly hard done by in all of this, but not so. **There are also special Tax Allowances in the Valencia region for surviving spouses who are living in Valencia at the time of the inheritance.** I have tried to research this particular aspect, as it is obviously of great importance to many people. Alas, I have been unable to find a firm response on whether the exemption now applies to non-residents or, for that matter, Spanish residents who live outside Valencia.

At first sight, it would seem obvious that surviving spouse allowances must apply to residents and non-residents alike, otherwise there is discrimination. However, it must be born in mind that the *national* legislation refers back to the local law of the various Autonomous Communities, and viewed from this point of view it is entirely possible that Valencian rules are applicable and therefor the surviving spouse has to be fiscally resident for 5 years before inheriting. As I have been unable to disentangle this one, I suggest as strongly as possible that you seek an expert opinion from your legal or financial representative, on where the law lies in this area.

In any event, roughly translated from the legalese, the rule regarding surviving spouses' states that if both you and your husband or wife has lived in Valencia and both have been registered to pay tax here for a 5 year period before the taxable event happened, the surviving spouse can take advantage of the extra allowance.

So, in addition to the allowances set out above, for the *surviving spouse who has been resident for 5 years in Valencia*, **the allowance against Inheritance Tax is €100,000, and a further discount of 75% is allowed on the actual tax payable**. Please, please check whether this may apply to you, if either either of you are not resident, or one of you is not resident, in Valencia.

Obviously, this is a very complex and very expert field, and I have done no more than scratch the surface here, to give you an idea of what to expect. To get a definitive picture of your own case, I urge you strongly to speak to your Financial Expert or Abogado, preferably before the issue arises! Don´t just use this as the definitive answer to all things Inheritance Tax; it isn´t, and I am not a Spanish lawyer. This area is intended to give you an outline of the Spanish inheritance tax situation, and no more. Basically, it´s only meant to let you know how complex the issue is, and to raise your awareness of the issues involved. Each individual case is different, and you **must** consult your own legal representative to get a definitive answer regarding your own liability.

But at least there really is a great deal of good news for you, in terms of where your Spanish assets can go, if you are not resident. Far better than giving a huge slice to the Tax Man.

And even better, there are ways of - legally - protecting your inheritance. As always, **please** speak to your legal representative/financial expert before going down this route, but as a matter of interest you may wish to be aware of the following:

❖ Generally, Spanish inheritance law limits who you can leave your assets to. This is to protect the family and provide for younger "children" (generally under the age of 21, unless they are disabled when different rules apply).

❖ You may wish to consider something called a "usufruct". In Spain this is where a beneficiary, normally the surviving spouse, is left a 'life interest' over assets, generally the family home, rather than a direct share of the property. This is intended to ensure that the surviving spouse will always, and quite literally, "have a roof over their head" for their lifetime. Again, this is not clear whether this applies to non-residents as well as residents. Although I have strong doubts about whether it can apply to non-residents, don´t take my word for it: sorry - yet something else to talk to your Abogado about.

- ❖ Using an usufruct can also reduce Spanish inheritance tax. By leaving the spouse a usufruct, full ownership of the house can eventually pass to the children without further tax at that stage, and in the meantime the surviving spouse can live in the property free for the rest of their lifetime.

As always, it´s not straightforward and you must, must, must take legal advice to ensure that this is all clear (and properly worded so it is legal!) in your Spanish will. More about the technicalities of wills in Spain later. You have got a Spanish will haven´t you? If not, get one now! If you don´t the amount of hassle and legalities you will be faced with should either you or your partner die will be unthinkable. Things get particularly complicated if, say, you have re-married and have step-children.

And there are even whole rafts of companies out there who will be delighted to help you to reclaim any inheritance tax that you may have already paid, as a non-resident legatee. As I have no idea of the credentials of any of them, if this applies to you I suggest typing in "Reclaiming Spanish Inheritance Tax" into your internet browser, and see what comes up! Many are Spanish firms with what appears to be a slightly sub-standard grasp of English, although they no doubt do know their business in this area. Others are English-speaking but based in Spain. Charging basis varies from company to company, but as the EU legislation is unequivocal you should - with a little help from your selected expert - experience not too much difficulty in getting your money back.

But as always, a couple of words of warning.

If you don´t apply for a refund, it´s not going to be volunteered! And whichever company you run with, do take care to take up references and financial bona fides.

Chapter 13

Changes to Income Tax Regulations for Residents

Good and bad news here, for residents, at least. Sorry, you still have to pay income tax to the Spanish authorities, but at far more advantageous rates than formerly.

The very good news is that from the 2015/2016 tax year (i.e. the amount you will be taxed on when you submit your return before June 2016, for the previous year), the basic taxable allowance will be around €12,000. The statement from the Government has been that anybody who is resident in Spain, and earns (including earnings via pensions whether public and private, paid either from the Spanish authorities or the UK authorities, or anywhere else in the world as long as they are taxed here in Spain) less than €12,000 per annum will pay no personal income tax.

❖ **Income Tax**

The following information on personal tax bands and allowances is accurate as at **the end of December 2015,** i.e. these are the rates you will pay when you make your declaration in June 2016.

Taxable Allowances as at 2015

This is per person, not per couple.

For the 2015 tax year (**you will pay tax for this year this in 2016**), income tax without age related personal allowances is banded as follows (these figures are purely for Valencia; it varies from Autonomous region to region. Valencia is definitely one of the best.)

Valencia	State	Region	Total 2015
€0 - €12,450	10%	11.9%	21.9%
€12,450 - €17,707.20	12.5%	11.9%	24.4%
€17,707.20 - €20,200	12.5%	13.92%	26.42%
€20,200 - €33,007.20	15.5%	13.92%	29.42%
€33,007.20 - €35,200	15.5%	18.45%	33.95%
€35,200 - €53,407.20	19.5%	18.45%	37.95%
€53,407.20 - €60,000	19.5%	21.48%	40.98%
€60,000 - €120,000	19.5%	21.48%	40.98%

€120,000 - €175,000	23.5%	22.48%	45.98%
Over €175,000	23.5%	23.48%	46.98%

If you are resident in Valencia and have children who live with you here, you will also get additional tax allowances for them. I do realise that you would have to be taking very early retirement indeed if this is applicable, but I have had feedback to indicate that retirees' age is getting younger and younger, so it is included for information. These are the applicable figures for tax years up to 2014; apologies, at the time of writing comparable figures for tax years after 2014 are not yet available.

Child allowance

First child	2,400 Euros
Second child	2,700 Euros
Third child	4,000 Euros
Each further child	4,500 Euros

So far so good! However, there is also a bit of rather less good news.

Up until the 2014/2015 tax year, the Spanish Tax Man was simply not interested in Civil Service pensions. These are pensions accruing from employment in the British Civil Service, the Armed Forces etc - **not** UK State "old age" Pensions. If you were in receipt of a Civil Service pension in any form, then you submitted this to the

UK tax authorities to be taxed (or at least you did if you had any sense, as effectively this gave you double tax free allowances).

Alas, this has now changed.

Beginning with the 2014/2015 tax year, you will have to submit your UK P60 for any Civil Service pension you are in receipt of. You will not be taxed on it in Spain, if you declare it to the UK Tax Authorities. **But** the Spanish Tax Authorities will take it into account when deciding your tax band. If you still do not earn in excess of your personal tax allowance, you will stay pay no tax. If you still fall into the lowest tax band, taking into account your Civil Service pension, then you will still pay the basic rate. If, however, the Civil Service pension pushes you into a higher tax band, then whatever amount falls into that band will be taxed at the higher rate. For instance, if you were earning €5,000 from a company pension last year, together with €10,000 from a Civil Service pension which was taxed in the UK, then you paid no Spanish income tax. This year - and for all succeeding years - the Hacienda will add your Civil Service pension to your already declared pension, and would say that you were earning €15,000 and as a result would be liable to pay the basic rate tax on the total amount that was not liable to tax.

The Hacienda states that they will take your Civil Service pension into account, i.e. they will add it to all other declared earnings. Once they have calculated what tax band this pushes you in to, they will then deduct your Civil Service pension from the actual taxable amount payable. In practice, it still means you are likely to pay more income tax. In my own case, I have gone from paying €48 in income tax last year, to €1,198 this year, thanks to a moderate Civil Service pension that is already declared to the UK tax authorities. Ouch.

I should add that there has been some dispute as to whether your P60 for the 2014/2015 tax year has to be submitted, or whether this will not come into effect until the 2015/2016 tax year. My own accountant told me very firmly to submit this year, in order to avoid undue hassle next year, so like a good little tax payer I did so. A neighbour was incensed when I mentioned it to him, as his accountant had not spoken to him about it. In either event, submit in 2016 or take the consequences; the Hacienda does talk to the UK tax authorities, and although no sanctions for non-submission have been disclosed yet, I have no doubt they will be there before long.

The Spanish Tax Authorities are insisting that this does not amount to taxing Civil Service pensions, as they will not deduct tax from them, just use them to calculate your banding.

I hear what they say, but it sounds remarkably like "back door" taxation to me. But apparently it has been agreed with the British tax authorities, who have allowed it under the dual taxation agreements.

Sorry, looks like we're stuck with it.

Chapter 14

Age Related Tax Advantages

There may not be a lot to be said for getting older, but at least this is one thing that is good in terms of paying less here in Spain. Basically, if you are resident here for tax purposes, then the older you get the less income tax you pay, at least up to a limit. There is also some good news if you have elderly relatives living with you, or young children who are your descendants.

At the time of writing, I cannot find the applicable figures for older tax payers but I have asked an expert in this area and the answer is that they cannot find any reason to expect that the "normal" additional allowances will not be applicable in addition to these figures. So, to give you some guidance on (hopefully) what can be expected as age-related extra allowances, the age related allowances **for tax years up to 2014 were**:

Personal allowance

Under 65 years old	5,550

(basic personal allowance for all tax payers)	Euros*
65+	6,700 Euros
75+	8,100 Euros

* See preceding chapter; now raised to approx. €12,000

At the other end of the scale, if you have what are officially described as "ascendants" living with you (which in English means parents and grandparents) then you will also receive taxable allowances for them. For the 2015 tax year, these are:

Ascendants 65 -75 who do not have a taxable income themselves : €918

Over 75: €2040

Worth noting that the allowances are payable for **any ascendant of any age** who lives with you and is graded as having a disability of 33% or more.

❖ **Annuities**

You might guess that the situation regarding annuities is different in Spain to that of the UK. Given the recent changes to drawing down annuities from pension scheme pots in the UK, this is an area that more and more would-be ex-pats are finding of great interest.

The good news? Generally, annuities are taxed favourably in Spain!

The latest information (as of summer 2015) is as follows.

1. In Spain, only a **proportion** of the **income** from your hard-earned annuity is treated as what is described as "non-taxable capital" with only the balance remaining being subject to income tax. I do apologise, but like most things tax related it is not straightforward. If you are considering bringing an annuity to Spain, to be taxed under Spanish law, **please** ensure that you take expert advice from a Spanish registered taxation expert. This is your money; you must be sure that you make the very best you can of it.

In outline (and very basically, just to give you an idea) this is the way it works:

a) The Hacienda works out the **taxable income** part of your annuity by applying a fixed percentage (between 40% and 8%) to the amount you have received in your "pot". This depends on your age **at the time the annuity is drawn down**. Bear in mind that this will never change, no matter how long you live; the amount of tax you pay (unless, of course, legislation changes the figures) will always depend on the age you were when you drew down your annuity. Not surprisingly, the older you are when you draw down your annuity, then the less tax you will pay on it here in Spain.

b) The rate varies widely, depending on how old you are at the time of draw down. As an example if you are under 40 (lucky you!) at the time you take your annuity, then you will expect to have **40%** of your annuity income taxed. Still leaves you with 60% not subject to tax! At the other end of the scale, if you are 70 or over when you draw down your annuity, only **8%** of your annuity income will be taxed, giving you a staggering **92%** of your annuity income tax free.

c) Actual rates of taxation are worked out on the basis of "savings income". At present (summer 2015), this means that the tax bands on the amount you pay are as follows

First €6,000 of taxable annuity: 20%

Between €6,000 - €50,000 - 22%

Above €50,000 - 24%

Worth noting that this preferential tax treatment applies, basically, only to your "pension pot" annuity, i.e. it is not applicable to annuities which you have acquired through inheritances, legacies etc. or where an employer has not contributed to your fund.

2. There is also a different approach for what are called "temporary annuities", i.e. an annuity which is not paid until your death, but which is only to be paid for a set period. In this case, the percentage of income which is taxable depends on how long the annuity is payable for. For a 5 year annuity, you would be liable for tax on 12% of the income. For an annuity of 15 years duration or longer, then 25% of the income is taxed.

So far, all good news. Unfortunately, there is still one area that is not entirely clear. This is - and I can only apologise for the bad news as this is probably the most common area where an annuity will arise - where the annuity accrues from **a private pension**.

Hacienda may treat this differently on the grounds that normally, in a private pension scheme, the Trustees of the scheme purchase an annuity on your behalf. As you are still the beneficiary of the annuity income, why this should make a difference is beyond me.

Anyway, if you state on your annual tax return that the private pension annuity **is** an annuity, it should be accepted as such, even though you did not purchase it yourself. If you do not claim for your annuity in this way, or if for some reason the Hacienda decides it is not a valid annuity, then none of the preferential provisions set out above will apply, and your annuity income will be taxed as general income at the normal rates.

Yet another excellent reason to get a good accountant/financial advisor on board, well before you make your first Spanish tax return!

❖ **Pension Lump Sums**

Just as in the UK and other EU and non-EU countries, pension lump sums are taxed in Spain. Obviously, they will only be taxed in Spain if you receive them while you are resident in Spain for tax purposes.

As always, the approach to taxation is different in Spain to that in the UK and other EU and non-EU countries. Because of this, it is well worth taking a look to see if you would be better off taking your lump-sum under Spanish legislation, or in your country of origin.

The way it works in Spain is this:

The taxable amount from your lump is calculated by the Hacienda as the difference between the actual amount you receive as you lump sum (the "capital amount") and the contributions you have made to that capital amount. Whatever the difference is, you will be taxed at the normal savings rates on that amount. This could make a huge difference to the amount you actually receive, so well worth deciding whether it would be beneficial to you to take your lump-sum before you move to the Costa Blanca!

I know it´s complicated, but at least it gives you have some idea of where the most beneficial place for your pension pot will be.

Chapter 15

Spanish Wills

Made sure your non-Spanish will is up to date? Drawn up a Spanish will as soon as your feet touched Costa Blanca soil? Good for you! You would be amazed how many people just never get round to it. And are you absolutely sure that all your wills world-wide are up to date? Recent legislation has made it all the more important that this is the case.

Why?

Well, firstly it´s a matter of common sense. If you have ever tried to disentangle somebody's legacy - no matter where in the world - where they have died without actually leaving a will, you will understand perfectly what I´m talking about. And yes, I do speak from personal experience. If somebody dies intestate (i.e. without leaving a valid will) then it can be a nightmare getting everything sorted out. Even if everything is straightforward and there is only one legatee, it still takes time and effort. Imagine, then, what the situation would be like if Aunty Sara died without leaving a will regarding who she wanted her Spanish property (and of course, in this context "property" means any asset that is physically sited in Spain; house, money in the bank, car….) to go to. Not only are you likely to be not perfectly fluent in "legal" Spanish, but you have no idea of how the legal system works. You can, and no doubt will, appoint a Spanish *Abogado* to deal with everything for you, but in the absence of a nice, straightforward will the amount of paperwork you will be expected to produce will be devastating, and all the time you are struggling to find everything, the clock will be ticking down to the day that the Hacienda demands their share …..

Make that will. Now! Never mind about the fact that you will not be here to see the chaos that ensues when you are gone. If you hate your relatives that much, you have no business leaving them anything in the first place. Give it all to charity instead (and more on that later).

And if you live in Spain but have any assets at all outside Spain, you also need a will which states clearly where these non-Spanish assets are to be disposed.

Sorry, I know. It is awkward, but far less awkward than it will be if you don´t take the time and relatively small expense in getting it right.

This is particularly so as from 2015, as the legislation regarding the disposal of assets in your will has changed. But before I move on to the new legislation, and how it affects you, I need to talk a little about the technical side of making a will in Spain.

Worth saying at the outset; expats of any nationality who live in Spain and who die here without having made a will **are subject to over-riding Spanish legislation.** Basically, this means that no matter how you really wanted to leave your estate, the Government will decide for you and will divide your assets according to Spanish law. In essence, this means that the "law of compulsory heirs" (ley de herederos forzosos) will be enforced. This law states that, should you die intestate in Spain (without leaving a valid will), the surviving spouse will automatically be entitled to all assets that were acquired before your marriage took place, together with half of all assets that were acquired during the marriage together with any personal gifts and inheritances made directly to them. There is more complexity to come, but think about just this area. Have you ever seen such a recipe for squabbles and contention? How, exactly, is your wife/husband going to prove that you really did gift him/her with all those shares in Iberdrola (which are still, of course, in your sole name), not to mention the car etc, if you haven´t made a will saying so? Not good. Do not go there. Make a Spanish will.

And if children (children are designated as "issue" under the age of 21, or of any age if they are officially categorized as "handicapped") are involved, it all gets infinitely worse. If the deceased has children, then the remainder of the estate after the surviving spouse has proved what he/she is entitled to is divided into three sections. **One third** is left to the children. If you have only one child, then they get the whole of this third. If you have two, three, four or even ten children, then this third is divided equally between them, no matter if it means they only get a negligible amount each. The **second third** is also destined for the children, but the assets passed on in this third **cannot be disposed of until after the surviving spouse has died**. All of which leaves yet another third. This final third of the estate can be passed to anybody (but then again, if you or your surviving spouse hasn't made a valid will, who knows where you wanted it to go?). If there are no children then **surviving parents of the deceased,** if any, are automatically entitled to that share of the estate.

Got all that?

Easier to make a will in Spain for your Spanish assets? You betcha! And this may well be the place to clear up a common misconception. You can, if you want to, try and cover how you want to leave your Spanish assets in a will which is both drawn up in, and is governed by, the law of your home country. I've often heard people say that they have done this, and so have no need to bother with a separate Spanish will. Nothing to stop you doing it, but there are some drawbacks. Firstly, if you dispose of your Spanish assets in, say an English will, you will have to wait for probate to be completed in England before proceedings can even begin in Spain. And of course, your English will must be translated into Spanish and notarized as being legally correct before you can dispose of a single asset. And if you do get it wrong, there will be a Spanish lawyer waiting with open arms to sort out your problems. At a price. All in all, cheaper and easier to get a Spanish will and have done with it.

Just to make things go with even more of a swing, there are several different types of will in Spain. And you must make sure that each one is drawn up in accordance with the relevant regulations. If you do not, then the will may be declared void and you are back to the nightmare scenario of dividing your assets according to Spanish legislation as outlined above.

The types of will valid in Spain are:

❖ **An open will (testament abierto)**. This is the most common type of will used. As with most wills it is not essential to get a lawyer to draft this for you; you can do it yourself. But you need to be absolutely sure that you are perfectly fluent in Spanish and that you have adhered to all the formalities if you go down the "do it yourself" route, otherwise you may find your heirs are faced with some nasty surprises. A notary can draw up this type of will for you (unlike the usual "lawyer **and** notary situation") and you will need three witnesses. The witnesses and the notary must sign the will and the person who is having the will drawn up will then be given a copy. Another copy is registered with the general registry of wills located in Madrid. The original is kept at the office of the notary and will be written in Spanish, although I would strongly suggest asking for a translation, to make sure the contents are totally as you wish. Cost? Around €180 - €200 at the time of writing.

❖ **A closed will (testament cerrado)** is one where the contents are not known to anyone apart from the testator and the lawyer. The will is then sealed in an envelope, and the envelope is then signed by two witnesses and the lawyer himself. The will is then registered in the same way that an open will is. I´m not at all sure why anybody would want this sort of will, unless it is to create a perpetual state of hopefulness amongst potential heirs! It´s certainly not common, but it you want to go down this route, it is available to you.

❖ The third type of will is **a holographic will (testament olografo)** and this is essentially the same beast as a holographic will under English law. It is written either by hand by the testator (the person who is leaving the estate) or is recorded orally. A written version needs to be signed and dated by the testator and must be clearly legible. You do not need witnesses and the testator is able to register the will themselves with the central registry in Madrid if they want to. An **oral will** must have **five witnesses** who must also testify before a notary about the wishes of the testator. The notary will draw up a written will to reflect the oral wishes and will certify it. For obvious reasons, an oral will is never to be recommended; and in any event, as it means even more fuss to get it ratified, why bother? Like its cousin in English law, a holographic may sound alright, but it can be forged and it´s far from unknown for mistakes to be made by the testator.

Unlike English and Scottish law, it is unusual to have an Executor named in a Spanish will, but nothing to stop you doing so! This is especially important for us ex-pats, who may feel we need a local, Spanish speaking Executor anyway. Be warned; if you name and appoint a lawyer to do this job they are able to charge up to 5% of the value of the estate as a fee. It´s more common for beneficiaries of an estate to use a local Abogado to do the leg-work for them. To do this, your beneficiaries must be able to produce either an original copy or an authorized copy of the death certificate before the estate can be processed. Any inheritance tax bill needs to be cleared within six months of the date of death although extensions can be applied for. Worth noting that assets are not officially released until the inheritance tax bill is paid.

And just as in many countries, when an estate is being processed in Spain it can take some time to complete. Be prepared to nag, and keep on querying your legal advisor for action.

And extremely importantly, you should be aware that the legal situation with regard to wills and probate has **changed recently** here in Spain. As always, it´s not an entirely simple situation but fortunately there is a very easy solution. There have also been a large amount of scare stories in the English speaking press, some grossly inaccurate, that have sparked considerable panic amongst ex-pats. Please don´t worry; the situation is now potentially beneficial for ex-pats resident in Spain, and the action needed to protect yourself is easily done.

The current situation is now:

The changes are applicable from 17 **August 2015,** as a result of new EU legislation. The Legislation states:

> *"EU citizens habitually residing in Spain (Residents) will be subject to the Spanish succession law, despite their nationality, unless they specifically state in their will the wish for the succession law of their country of origin to apply."*

Please note that the legislation **only applies to Spanish residents.** I have seen a number of advertisements for Abogados which are worded to suggest that non-resident expats are also captured. **This is not the case.**

The most important changes are:

❖ The regulation **does not directly have an effect on UK, Republic of Ireland or Danish nationals**, as the legislation is not enacted in these countries. This means that if you are a national of any of these countries, **you must take specific action to enable the legislation**. Not at all as scary as it sounds; see below.

❖ If you are a national of the UK, Republic of Ireland or Denmark, if you wish Spanish succession law to apply to your will (for details see the preceding chapter) then to avoid any doubt you should add a clause to your Spanish will stating that you want Spanish law to apply.

❖ If you wish the succession law of your "native" country to apply (e.g. if you wish to leave everything to your wife, and nothing to your children, or the whole lot to a second cousin, none of which is allowable under

Spanish law) then you **must** ask your Abogado to add a clause into your **Spanish** will stating that you want **the law of the UK, Ireland or Denmark to apply** (as the case may be) to your inheritance. If you do this then you can allocate your estate as you wish, providing it is legal under the law of your country of origin. And that is all you need to do. But bear in mind, if you go down this route then the laws regarding inheritance allowances in Spain still apply - see the table for allowances against inheritance tax.

For the avoidance of doubt - and there has been plenty of confusion over this area - the new legislation applies only to succession planning in your will. Some people appear to hope it means that they can get out of Spanish law entirely, by applying the law of say, England and Wales to their will. Sorry, it doesn´t work like that! No matter whom you choose to leave your inheritance to, you will still be subject to normal Spanish taxation for your Spanish estate, as set out in the inheritance allowance tables.

Also a bit more good news. Before the new legislation, it was quite difficult to leave money to charities in Spain, as all inheritances had to be made to a named individual. Now, if you want your inheritance to be distributed under English and Welsh law (and I assume it is a similar procedure under Scottish law? If it isn´t, please do put me right) you are perfectly at liberty to nominate a charity rather than an individual, but please bear in mind that inheritance tax will still be payable under Group 4.

And the last word on the subject of wills. Whilst you can, or at least in theory, draft your Spanish will to include the disposal of assets outside of Spain, it is generally desirable to have two wills - one for your Spanish assets and (assuming you have assets outside of Spain, of course) one executed in the country where your other assets are sited, specifically for those assets. So, if you have money in the bank in the UK or any other asset in the UK or outside Spain, get English will that covers it. Much easier, especially at a time when the last thing your heirs want is yet more confusion.

Chapter 16

UK State Benefits Payable to Spanish Residents

You may be amazed how many UK state benefits are still claimable by you, even though you are resident in Spain. This is a short run down of what is out there, although of course these will depend on your individual situation.

If you think you may be eligible for any of them then contact the relevant Government department for full information. I have given a hyperlink for each area, wherever possible.

Prime amongst the list is, of course, your state pension. If you are already in receipt of your state pension in the UK, or have a date when you will be eligible to receive it, then you can also receive it here on the Costa Blanca. You can elect to have it paid into a bank or building society in the UK, or paid to your bank here in Spain.

If you are already in receipt of your state pension before you move here, you must contact the International Pensions Center (IPC) to advise them of your change of residence - (**Error! Bookmark not**

defined. Telephone: +44 (0)191 218 7777) - get in touch as soon as you are sure of your moving date, in case of delay.

If you have not yet reached pension age, then you must still inform IPC that you are moving and give them all your new address details. They will then send you a letter giving you details of your pension at least 3 months before you are due to receive it. If you don't receive your letter by the due date, then contact them asap.

If you want to work out what your state pension is going to be, it's worth a visit to http://www.gov.uk/calculate-state-pension.

And just in case you've missed it somewhere along the way, the UK State Pension is changing. The changes will apply to you if your are:

a man born on or after 6 April 1951

a woman born on or after 6 April 1953

Check your eligibility on https://www.gov.uk/state-pension.

If you were born before these dates, you can check your pension situation at https://gov.uk/state-pension.

If you need to get in touch with them, you can contact the IPC by email or phone, or fill in the link at http://www.gov.uk/government/publications/guidance-on-claiming-a-state-pension-if-you-retire-abroad.

You'll need the international bank account number (IBAN) and bank identification code (BIC) numbers for your overseas account.

And I´m afraid that your UK state pension will have to be declared to the Hacienda, and you will be taxed on it (assuming you earn more than the personal tax allowance) here in Spain.

You may also be able to claim **bereavement benefit from the UK Government.** I often find myself starting information about living in Spain with the words "It´s complicated" but since delving into the UK Government websites for this information, I´ve realised that bureaucracy is complex the world over!

So, here goes. There are **three** types of Bereavement Benefits that you may be able to claim if you are a UK national resident in Spain. All must be claimed **within 3 months of losing your wife, husband or civil partner.**

❖ The **State Bereavement Payment** is a tax free lump-sum of £2,000 that may be payable if you are under State Pension age when you lost your partner, or if your deceased partner wasn't entitled to Category A State Retirement Benefit when they died. (Contact HMRC Residency Helpline 0044 191 203 7010 for the ins and outs of it). I should add that it is wise to check with your Abogado if this lump-sum is taxable in Spain; the website is silent on this and I have not been able to prise an answer out of anybody about it.

❖ In addition, you may be able to claim **Bereavement Allowance.** This is a taxable weekly benefit paid for up to 52 weeks if you aged 45 or over at the time of death, you are not bringing up children, you are under State Pension age and your husband, wife or partner paid National Insurance contributions or died as a result of an accident or disease through work.

It's not clear who to contact for this from abroad as the claim is through Jobcentreplus – Department for Work and Pensions. If it applies to you, I suggest ringing the HMRC helpline for clarification.

❖ **Widowed Parent's Allowance** is payable when you have a dependent child or person aged 16-20 for whom you receive Child Benefit, you are under State Pension age and your husband, wife or partner paid National

Insurance contributions. Again, ring HMRC helpline for details.

You may also be able to claim **Disability Living Allowance**

Again, there are three benefits which may be available for ex-pats resident in Spain:

- ❖ **Disability Living Allowance (DLA)**
- ❖ **Carer's Allowance (CA)**
- ❖ **Attendance Allowance (AA)**

These may be claimed if you or a family member that you are dependant on pays national insurance contributions in the UK, you receive UK State Pension / Bereavement Benefit / UK Sickness Benefit and you have spent 26 of 52 weeks in the UK on the date that you claim. (Contact International Pension Center Telephone: 0044 191 218 7777; Email TVP.internationalqueries@thepensionservice.gsi.gov.uk). Apologies for the dreadful jargon in this section; this is the way it´s set out on the Government website, and no amount of digging has unearthed anything that makes it any clearer. The best advice I can give is that if you think you may be eligible, then ring IPS or send them an e-mail asking for clarification.

You may also be able to claim **Industrial Injuries Disablement Benefit,** if you are ill or disabled as a result of an accident that happened at work. The accident that caused your disability must have happened in England, Scotland or Wales. You need to have been employed at the time of the accident and it must have happened in England, Scotland or Wales. It doesn't help greatly that claims are only processed by one of two Industrial Injuries Disablement Benefit centers, each of which can only be contacted either by telephone or post.

Details of these centers are:

Barrow Benefit Center
Post Handling Site B
Wolverhampton
WV99 1RX

Telephone: 0345 603 1358
Textphone: 0345 608 8551

Barnsley IIDB Center
Mail Handling Site A
Wolverhampton
WV98 1SY

Telephone: 0345 758 5433
Textphone: 0345 608 8551

What used to be called **Incapacity Benefit / Employment and Support Allowance** can also be claimed by Spanish residents. Incapacity Benefit applications ceased in early 2011, but you can continue to claim this from Spain if it is already being paid to you. Employment and Support Allowance is paid if you have a disability or illness that prevents you from working. For this, you should have paid national insurance contributions in the UK within 3 years of your claim. (For details contact International Pension Center).

Personally, I find the next one amazing but if you qualify for it, it is your right to claim it.

Job Seekers Allowance. You may be able to claim up to three months of contribution-based Job Seekers Allowance (JSA) if you have registered as a job seeker for at least a month before you leave the UK, you are available for work in the UK up to the day you leave, you are going abroad to look for work or you are entitled to the benefit on the day you leave. Apply online at https://.dwpe-services.direct.gov.uk/portal/page/portal/jsaol/lp.

If your claim is successful, you must take an E303 form from your local job center in the UK to the Instituto Nacional del Empleo office in Spain. You will then need to sign on in Spain within a week of arrival to receive your benefit payments and you must continue to visit the office every three months to register as looking for work.

And finally, one benefit that has recently ceased to be payable. HM Government has decided, in its infinite wisdom, that those of who live on the Costa Blanca can´t possible have cold winters, so the Winter Fuel Payment has now ceased to exist.

If you think you may be eligible for any of the benefits outlined above, contact the relevant department to find out what you need to do to claim it. But please remember, you must also speak to your tax advisor to find out if any or all of the benefits will be taxable in Spain.

Chapter 17

The Final Chapter - Dying in Spain

I thought I had covered this in Volume 1. But judging by the amount of feedback I have received, a great deal more information would be welcome for ex-pats living - and intending to end their lives - here in the Costa Blanca.

Not a topic any of us want to consider, but it´s even more necessary in Spain - with the differences in the way things are done and the language barrier - than it is in your native country. Because it´s something that happens so rarely to an individual's friends and family, everything is unfamiliar. And of course, making complex arrangements are the last thing anybody wants to think about when they have just been bereaved.

So here goes; the basics of what needs to be done in the event of an ex-pat dying in the Costa Blanca.

❖   **Death at home**

I think this is the worst possible scenario. It assumes that a doctor was not present at the time of death. Once you have found the courage to continue, then you should, as soon as possible:

- ❖ Ring 112. This is the emergency number, and will always have an English or German speaker on line. Explain what has happened, and they will arrange for the *Juez Forense* (Coroner) to get to you as a matter of urgency. In practice, this may be a representative in the form of an attending doctor.

- ❖ The doctor will authorize the removal of the body, and will also issue you with a **medical death certificate**. This death certificate is vital, you cannot proceed without it.

- ❖ If you have a pre-paid funeral plan, ring the number for them. They all provide a 24 hour service, and normally included in the price is a full administration service. From this point on, they should help you through all the legalities.

- ❖ If you do not have a funeral plan, I am afraid you must contact a local *tanatorio* (funeral director) directly. I have given details of some English speaking tanatorios at the end of this chapter. If you don't have a clue - not surprising at a time like this - it is highly likely that the Juez Forense will be able to help you with details of a local firm. The funeral director, as with the pre-paid funeral plans, should be able and willing to help with all the admin. involved.

❖ **Death in hospital from "natural causes"**

A great deal easier in this case.

❖ If the deceased dies in hospital, then the hospital authorities will take care of the administrative details. But a word of warning; I know from personal experience that it is considered normal for the hospital authorities to alert a local tanatorio that the death has occurred. In practice, this means that you may well be introduced to a local funeral director before you can even get out of the hospital. If you already have a funeral plan, just explain this to them and they will smile and remove themselves. If you are happy for them to take things over for you (and of course, it can be a huge relief not to have make the arrangements for yourself) try, if you feel up to it, to find out what their costs are and what they are offering. If you are not happy, then go with another tanatorio, it´s entirely your choice.

❖ **"Judicial" Cases**

If death has occurred suddenly or is due to an accident:

❖ The police must be called at once (112 again) if they do not arrive automatically. The death will be deemed "judicial" (probably best rendered in English as "suspicious") if the *Juez Forense* or attending doctor is in any doubt as to the cause of death. In this case, I am afraid that - just as in most countries - an autopsy will be required. If this happens, the deceased will be taken to the nearest Forensic Institute (Instituto Anatómico Forense) (usually located in the nearest large town; very few villages or small towns will have their own) where an autopsy will be carried out to determine the cause of death.

❖ Once the cause of death has been established, you must apply to the court for the permit for the body to be released. Your tanatorio or funeral plan administrator may be willing to do this for you. If they are not, they should at the very least tell you what you need to do to get the permit. If all else fails, ask for advice from your Abogado, although I would hope that the need for this would be few and far between.

❖ You also need to be aware of the logistics where death has occurred outside the deceased home. Basically, what happens is:

    a)   In "judicial cases", the police will automatically call the local tanatorio. If the deceased has a pre-paid funeral plan, make sure you tell them! It's entirely possible that the funeral plan company uses a different tanatorio and you may find that the policy is void if an unlisted tanatorio is used. Don't forget, the funeral plan administrator will be contactable by telephone 24/7, so get in touch ASAP to avoid problems.

b)	If a person dies in hospital in a different municipality from where they normally lived and you want a local funeral director in the place in which they live to collect the body (or, of course, if you have a pre-paid funeral plan) then you must tell the hospital authorities or they will automatically call a local (to them) tanatorio for you.

c)	If you are not confident in your Spanish you may be happier to call in a tanatorio who you are sure speaks English. In any event, once you have appointed your tanatorio or got in touch with your funeral agent, they should liaise with all the necessary authorities for you. But do note that you must tell them what funeral arrangements you want (particular religion? Non-religious ceremony? Cremation? Ossuary?) and it's up to you to ensure that you know all the costs involved. Things tend to be done differently in Spain; for instance, in the UK you would probably find that the fee for the funeral service automatically includes the fee for a religious officiary. In Spain, this is often a separate fee, and can be quite expensive.

❖ **Paperwork**

Difficult in any country at a time of death, but even more so when everything is strange.

❖ Starting with **death certificates**.

You might have guessed, but in Spain there is not just one death certificate, but two.And to make matters worse, there are several different types of the Civil Registry Death Certificate available. And yes, both certificates are essential.

a)   The doctor who initially attends after the death will issue a **medical** death certificate. This only confirms the identification of the deceased and gives the cause of death.

b)   You also require the local **Civil Registry death certificate,** which you will obtain when you register the death.

❖ The next step is to **register the death.** In Spain, you can either do this personally, or by post or (in a few areas, definitely not all) by e-mail/internet at the nearest Civil Registry (*Registro Civil*). This **must be done within 24 hours of death occurring.** To register the death, you must present the medical death certificate. In the case of an autopsy only, the authorities concerned will present the medical death certificate and process the Civil Registry death certificate.

In addition to the medical death certificate, you must also produce the following at the Registry (or attach copies if you are applying by post/internet):

The name, surname and passport or Residencia details of the person requesting the certificate

The medical death certificate

Full details of the next of kin

The following information relating to the person who had died:

Name and surname

Names of the parents

Marital status

Nationality

Date of birth and where born

Passport number or DNI (National identification number)

Last known residence/address

Date, time and location of the death (as detailed in medical death certificate)

Desired place of burial/cremation, if known

Type of certificate you require (see below).

Your own contact details in case of query.

❖ **Civil Registry Death Certificates**

There are a number of variations of Spanish Civil Registry death certificates. These are:

1) The **Extract:** This is a shortened version which contains the basic information necessary to obtain the following certificates -

2) A**"normal"** Spanish death certificate (in Spanish);

3) The **Literal** certificate: this is a longer document with contains all the information relevant to the death. Not normally required for deaths in Spain. Should any organization want it they will advise you if is required.

4) The **International Death Certificate** (written in a number of languages including Spanish and English).

You will need a *normal* Spanish death certificate for Spanish bank accounts, life insurance policies and most other formal entities in Spain that need to be advised of the death, but an *International Certificate* is recommended for all non-Spanish entities.

The death certificate, issued by the local Registro Civil is usually available within two to three days and can be collected in person or be sent by post. In some towns it will be issued at the offices of the local Justice of the Peace (Juzgado de Paz). Remember to ask for as many original copies ("copias originales") as you will need, plus a few to be on the safe side. These are normally issued free of charge.

Generally, if the deceased was a British citizen, the following are likely to require a copy of the death certificate (I have given contact details below):

Registro Civil in Madrid

Probate Office, if a UK will exists, or if the deceased had property/assets in the UK

Department of Work and Pensions in the UK, if the deceased was receiving a British State Pension

Spanish Social Security (Instituto de Seguridad Social INSS), but only if the deceased had worked in Spain and/or was in receipt of a Spanish pension

Paymaster General, if the deceased received any payments from the UK Government or a UK company pension

Inland Revenue, if the deceased paid UK tax

All banks where the deceased held accounts

Any insurance companies which held life or endowment policies on the life of the deceased

Any private pension companies

I would strongly advise taking copies of all your Spanish "official" documents and passport as a matter of course - I have everything scanned and on the laptop, just in case.

Although there is no leeway in registering the death within 24 hours, it is well worth asking your tanatorio or funeral plan administrator if they can help with the process. If not, your Abogado will certainly be able to help, but will of course charge for it. If you really have to do it yourself, I would take an interpreter with me. My Spanish is reasonably good, but in a situation like a bereavement I just know that I would suddenly be unable to string a sentence together and there is no guarantee at all that the Registrar will speak anything but Spanish. Even if you cannot find all the necessary documents, go to the Registrar and take what you have got. At least that way, the process has started and the Registrar should be able to advise you where to go to obtain duplicates.

In addition to the above, if the deceased was a UK national, you may find it advantageous to **register the death with the British Consulate**. Although it should be noted that this is not compulsory. If you do, it will mean that a British death certificate is available and a record of the death will be held in the UK.

❖ To register the death **with the British Consulate** you will need:

Application form (available from the British Consulate offices or download from http://www.fco.gov.uk/Files/kfile/death/registrationform.pdf

The local death certificate from the Civil Registry

The deceased's passport or full British birth certificate

Take (or send by post) the above documents to the British Consulate-General in Madrid (see below for contact details) with the appropriate registration fee.

❖ **Making the Funeral Arrangements**

Finally, once all the red tape had been gone through, you can arrange the burial or cremation. Be warned! Normally, funerals are held very, very quickly in Spain, as is common in most hot countries. **Generally, within 24 - 48 hours of death.** You can ask for the funeral to be delayed to allow relatives to be informed and make travel arrangements, but this is expensive - mortuary space is charged per day.

When the funeral company/agent has been appointed, or your pre-paid funeral plan administrator informed, you must provide then with the deceased passport, together with your own, and the full names of the deceased parents.

Although all arrangements will be organised by the funeral company, you will have to decide on the details you want. This will be set out in a written contract which you must sign.

Should you want to repatriate the body to the deceased country of origin for burial, you can ask for this to be done but (unless it is already covered in the funeral plan) it is very expensive as the body has to be embalmed to a satisfactory level here in Spain, and is then transported in a lead coffin. Ashes may also be repatriated, for which the tanatorio will provide a certificate.

Here in Spain the dead are either cremated and the ashes given to the next of kin for disposal as they see fit, or the body is housed in a coffin in an ossuary, which is an above-ground niche. The latter are either purchased outright, or the niche rented. If you have a strong preference for either, it´s a good idea to make your wishes known, and if you want a niche in an ossuary make sure you leave sufficient funds to   pay for it!

❖   **English Speaking Funeral Directors**

The English Funeral Director
Costa Blanca South Only
Office: 968 956 409
Mobile: 650 631 719 (24Hrs)
Email: tony@englishfuneraldirector.com

Costa Blanca Funerals

0034 - 62 84 299 72 (24/7)
0034 - 966 79 08 94
Website: http://www.costablancafuneral.com/EN/welcome.htm

International Funeral Services

Alicante area

965 142 597

Website: http://www.viva-
alicante.com/international_funeral_services_p30153.php

Grupo ASV Servicios

All of Costa Blanca

965 205 444

http://www.grupoasvserviciosfunerarios.com/en/ubicaciones/

Rowland Brothers International

Repatriation services only

44 (0)208 684 2324/Emergency Telephone: +44 (0)208 684 2324
Email: info@rowlandsbrothersinternational.com
Website: http://www.rowlandbrothersinternational.com

Tanatorio Crematorio-Javea

965 790 188

Appendix 1

USEFUL CONTACTS

International Pension Center

Tel.: +44 191 218 7777

Fax: +44 191 218 7381

Website: http//:www.thepensionservice.gov.uk/ipc/home.asp

Email: internationalqueries@thepensionservice.gsi.gov.uk

HM Paymaster General

Tel: +44 1293 604 546 (switchboard)

Email: opgservice@paymaster.co.uk

Inland Revenue

Tel.: +44 151 210 2222

Probate Helpline Tel.: +44 845 3020 900

Spanish Social Security Institute (Instituto de Seguridad Social (INSS)

Tel.: 900 16 65 65/901 50 20 50

Ministry of Justice (Ministerio de Justicia)

Customer helpline: 902 007 214

Website: http://www.mjusticia.es

Register Offices in Spain (to register births, marriages and deaths)

Website: http://registradores.org/en/index.jsp

British Consulate-General

Tel.: 91 524 97 00
Fax: 91 524 97 30
Email: mailto:madridconsulate@fco.gov.uk

Age Concern España

Website: **Error! Bookmark not defined.**
For further information ring INFOLINE on (+34) 902 00 38 38 or
send an email to info@ageconcern-espana.org

Iberdrola (electricity supply)

www.iberdrola.es

Healthcare in Valencia

www.san.gva.es

Driving in Spain

www.n332.es

Acknowledgements

With grateful thanks to:

UK Government Foreign and Colonial Office

British Consulate Alicante

Age Concern Spain

HM Passport Office

Blevins Franks

Expat Forum

SpainExpat

Perez Legal Group

White and Baos Abogados

HR Services, Moraira

Driving in Spain - N332

Tráfico, Alicante

Disclaimer

Please note that I am not professionally qualified in Spain to give legal, financial or taxation information here on the Costa Blanca. I was, before I retired, a Chartered Company Secretary and legal draftsman, so (unless my brain has rotted more than I think it has) I have a reasonable grasp of all things legal. Be that as it may, I often find myself frowning over the sheer complexity of Spanish legal affairs!

Rather, this Guide is intended as a fairly light-hearted introduction to retiring to the Costa Blanca, and as such is a compilation of my own experiences as an ex-pat living on the Costa Blanca, and information obtained from a wide variety of sources. The information contained in this Guide is intended for general guidance only. The application and impact of laws and regulations can vary widely from time to time and the application of them to you is based on your individual circumstances, of which I have no knowledge. Given the changing nature of laws, rules and regulations I cannot guarantee that there are no omissions or inaccuracies in information provided. Accordingly, the information in this Guide is provided on the understanding that the author is not engaged in rendering legal, accounting, tax, or other professional advice and services. As such, this Guide **must not** be used as a substitute for consultation with professional accounting, tax, legal or other competent advisers. Before making any decision or taking any action, you must consult the relevant professional.

Whilst I have used my best endeavours to ensure that the information contained herein has been obtained from reliable sources, I am not responsible for any errors or omissions, or for the results obtained from the use of this information. All information in this site is provided "as is", with no guarantee of completeness, accuracy, timeliness or of the results obtained from the use of this information, and without warranty of any kind, express or implied. In no event will I be liable to you or anyone else for any decision made or action taken in reliance on the information in this Guide or for any consequential, special or similar damages howsoever these may arise.

Certain links in this site connect to other websites maintained by third parties over whom I have no control. Because of this, I make no representations as to the accuracy or any other aspect of information contained in other websites.

If you enjoyed Volume 2 of "Dreaming of Retiring to the Costa Blanca?", you might also like to try:

Need a New Knee? Don´t Panic!

A Self-Help Manual for Before, During and After Your Knee Replacement Operation

Yvonne Bartholomew

I had a full knee replacement some 2 years ago – after 18 months of steadily increasing pain, and decreasing mobility. For the last few months, I could only walk with the aid of a walking stick, and was in constant pain, particularly at night. In spite of this, my surgeon's decision to operate took me by surprise – up until the moment he said "the time is right", he had insisted I was too young, too overweight… nice to be too young for something, but how did he expect me to lose weight when I could barely walk??? That, then, was my journey towards a new knee. And that is (almost) the last you will read about it here. This is not a personal diary, although it has arisen out of my own experience of a knee replacement. Rather, it is a manual. A manual that I hope will help other people avoid the problems I had. A manual that tells you the things you didn´t even know you should be asking, and is designed to help you through the process from the moment the surgeon says those momentous words – "You need surgery". A manual that will help you to gain peace of mind before, during and after surgery. A manual that will, I hope, help you through the process and recovery, and make that recovery quicker and easier than might otherwise have been the case.

Dreaming of Retiring to the Costa Blanca? Read This First! Vol.1
All the information you need to stop the Dream turning into a Nightmare

Yvonne Bartholomew

We moved to the lovely Costa Blanca North around nine years ago, and I can honestly say that we have had no regrets at all in leaving grey, cold, crowded England. Life here is as good as it gets; the weather is kind, the people lovely, the food and drink excellent, the whole lifestyle an object lesson in how life should be lived. Sounds wonderful? Take my word for it, it is!

Before we moved, I thought I had done as much research as it was possible to do. I thought I had all the answers at my fingertips; and bear in mind I used to work for the British Library, so if I couldn´t be confident that I had done my research well and thoroughly, who could? I read numerous "how to" guides, haunted the internet, made sure I kept up with all the Costa Blanca local papers on line. It was only after we had made the move, alas, that I realised that I had neglected the one, vital thing that **all** expats don´t understand, and it´s a real Catch-22 situation. You see, until you move, until you get over here and start settling in, you suddenly realise that whilst all that research is lovely, you still don´t have the key to **living** here.

Why? Simply because *you don´t know what the right questions are to ask!* You really do have to live here to know how true this simple fact is. The manuals and the internet articles are a help, of course, but they are far less than half the story. I soon found a thousand questions, and of course more importantly the answers to those questions – that were the things I wished I had known about before we packed our bags and left the UK to live in sunnier climes. Because, I am afraid, in laid-back Spain, if you don´t ask the correct question, you will either not get an answer at all (other than a shrug of the shoulders) or a good-natured stab at an answer that is likely to cause more confusion than anything else. At the very best, you will get an answer to the question you asked, but nothing else.

You will not be told that this is just part of a process, and there are lots more you need to do. Nothing will be volunteered, and if you don't know what the right question is, you will find yourself sinking rapidly. Unfortunately, bureaucracy in Spain is immense and unbending. Rules and regulations change regularly, and it can be a nightmare if you don't understand the basics. Once you understand the processes, it becomes second nature, and you stop worrying. It took me years to get to this stage! But you don't have to go through that process; everything I have learned the hard way is here.

And for when you just want a good read ....

Romancing the Rose
The Untold Story of England's Forgotten Queen
Yvonne Bartholomew

Everybody remembers Richard the Lionheart. The Crusader King. But who now remembers his Queen, Berengaria of Navarre? Wife of the greatest King in the whole of Christendom. Snatched from a certain future in a convent, when a grotesque twist of fate deprived Richard of the woman he should have married.

Married to the man she had worshiped for years. The King that everyone knew was the most respected warrior in Christendom; the greatest scholar; the courtliest lover. Berengaria's future happiness should have been certain. And yet ... her life was pure adventure from the moment she heard that she was to be Richard's bride. Shipwrecked and taken prisoner on her way to her own wedding; went with Richard to the Crusades and was forced to follow behind her King when his Crusade failed and the Holy Land fell to Saladin the Magnificent. Saw her beloved sister-in-law die in her arms. Betrayed by her husband, her lover, her friend. Overshadowed by her own mother-in-law, the great matriarch Eleanor of Aquitaine. Married to the legend that turned out to be a monster; a monster who broke her heart, but never her spirit.

Evicted from her beloved home by her own brother-in-law King John after Richard's pointless death. Doomed to a life of poverty and obscurity by John.

And in spite of everything that fate could throw at her, Berengaria was an icon of her age. The bravest, most tragic queen that England has ever known.

The only English queen never to set foot on English soil. England's lost queen.

Her story is magnificent, tragic, moving. It is a story that echoes down the 800 years since her death, and is as remarkable now as it was then.

It is a story of a remarkable woman, who lived in remarkable times.

A story that deserves to be told.

Remember Berengaria, for she deserves to be remembered.

The Costa Blanca News described "Romancing the Rose" as "The English Royal Family's best kept secret ... gripping".

Awarded 4**** by In d'Tale Magazine!

Shortlisted for a category award by the "RONE" Fiction Awards

All these books are available as an e-book on Kindle, or in hard copy on Amazon.

Happy reading!

11814179R00115

Printed in Great Britain
by Amazon.co.uk, Ltd.,
Marston Gate.